CO___ING

s Guide

Kate
Smedley
with
Archie
Braddock

I Issue.
8/2018.

Introduction

Are you looking for a hobby that will get you out of the house, improve your health and self-esteem, while stimulating your mind? Perhaps you are looking for a sport that doesn't require an initial expensive outlay or one that doesn't depend on the presence of other people for you to take part?

Coarse fishing gives you all of that and more. It is one of the most popular activities in the United Kingdom. You may be surprised to learn that between two and three million people regularly fish, making it the country's largest participant sport. It doesn't matter if you are seven or 70, male or female, a fanatic, advanced angler, a total beginner or a mad keen match angler – coarse fishing offers something for everyone.

This easy-to-read guide is written for anyone interested in taking up coarse fishing as a hobby. If you are a complete beginner with no idea which end of the rod you should hold to begin with, this book is written with you in mind. Full of relevant, expert advice, it will take you through the basics of what to wear, what type of tackle to use and provide in-depth tuition on how to use it.

In addition, this informative book details the different types of freshwater fish, how to catch them and the most effective baits to use, taking you through a typical day's fishing at a commercial fishery and other still waters, as well as a day's fishing on a river.

For those wishing to hone or improve their fishing skills, there are also sections written with you in mind. Two chapters are dedicated to advanced angling techniques, one focuses on flavoured baits, the second explores the world of after dark fishing, artificials and the effectiveness of the Big Fish Rig. Whatever level you are at, from complete novice to experienced angler, this book is packed with all the advice you need, together with countless invaluable tips to give you that angling edge.

Coarse fishing is unique. It is a pastime you can take up with relatively little financial outlay. Not only that, but you can go fishing as little or as often as you like, from once a month, to several times a week. You can choose to go alone, with your family or in a group; it's really up to you. You can opt to fish for pleasure or compete against other anglers. Coarse fishing is neither ageist, nor sexist. It is available and accessible to everyone, from the able to the not so able.

For young anglers, it offers a healthier alternative to whiling away the hours than being transfixed by the latest computer games or social media trends. It is without doubt more life-enhancing than roaming the streets, offering a new purpose and way of life to disaffected youngsters. One scheme launched in England aims to do just that and we provide information on that in the help list.

As many anglers will testify, the advantage of coarse fishing is that you can pursue your passion as far as you want to, but one thing is for certain. No two fishing trips are the same. The lone angler will relish the company of an array of birdlife, from robins, blackbirds and chaffinches to herons, great crested grebes, mallards, coots and waterhens. You may also be visited by kingfishers, kestrels, sparrowhawks and small mammals such as voles, weasels, escaped minks, mice and shrews.

From the time they reel in their first fish many anglers find themselves hooked, if you'll excuse the pun! The thrill of that first catch is a memory that lingers for a lifetime, spurring you on to catch more, and bigger, fish.

This easy-to-understand book takes you through a step-by-step guide providing all of the information you need to begin your new hobby. The experienced angler will not only be able to revise basic skills but learn unique advanced angling techniques. Please note that all product details and prices mentioned in this guide are correct at the time of writing.

Before you dip your toe in the water, however, there's something you should know . . . Coarse fishing can seriously benefit your health and improve your life.

Acknowledgements

While writing this book I was fortunate enough to have unlimited access to the advice and knowledge of one of the UK's most well-known and respected coarse anglers, my father, Archie Braddock.

With over sixty years' experience of fishing and responsible for launching his own line of bait flavours which still sell years after he officially retired, Archie has also written several popular books on fishing as well as contributing many chapters to specialist fishing books.

He has featured on the television programmes *Screaming Reels* and *Tight Lines*, Radio 5 Live and various videos and DVDs. He still provides occasional articles to monthly fishing magazines.

I am grateful for his unique insight and invaluable advice throughout this project and for the time spent on the riverbanks with him, testing out his intriguing theories and ideas – all of which work.

Special thanks

We would like to express our thanks to Dragon Carp Direct/Used Tackle for kindly providing many of the photographs used throughout the book.

Chapter One

What is Coarse Fishing?

Definition

Coarse fishing is angling in fresh water for non-migratory fish, known as 'coarse fish'. This excludes fishing for salmon, trout and other game fish and sea fish. Coarse fishing can take place on lakes, lochs, rivers, canals, gravel pits and ponds. Even the tiniest of farm ponds can hold fish well worth catching.

The benefits of coarse fishing

Coarse fishing brings with it numerous benefits, some of which you may find surprising:

- The simple act of being outside in the fresh air is recognised as having positive effects on your physical and mental health and boosts brain power. Vitamin D, which we get from sunshine, has been proven to positively affect our sense of wellbeing.

- It helps with weight management, improves self-esteem and reduces levels of anxiety and stress. Even a bad fishing day wins hands down over a day spent in the office or labouring on the factory floor.

- Anglers report a great sense of self-fulfilment while fishing. Coarse fishing enables you to learn new outdoor skills and often achieve long-held personal goals. All fishing requires a high level of self-discipline and patience which can contribute significantly to your personal and social development.

- Contrary to popular misconceptions, coarse fishing is not a sedentary sport – just ask anyone who regularly carries their fishing gear up and down the

'Contrary to popular misconceptions, coarse fishing is not a sedentary sport.'

riverbank. Surveys reveal that angling burns up to 490 calories per hour when actively fishing in waders. Sitting passively on the banks of the river burns almost 250 calories per hour. This compares favourably with activities such as dog-walking, volleyball and gentle canoeing. With concern over rising obesity across the UK, coarse fishing offers many weight management and health benefits.

- Coarse fishing can soon evolve into a lifelong activity, offering a constant learning environment. Many life lessons can be learned on the banks of a river or during a leisurely afternoon spent at a lake.

- Above all, fishing is fun! Once you've experienced the adrenalin surge of that first vanishing float, your inaugural battle with a reluctant fish, capturing it in the landing net and releasing it safely back into the water, you will begin to understand why the majority of anglers simply can't resist going back for more.

Do I need to buy a rod licence?

England and Wales

Everyone over the age of 12 requires a rod licence to fish in England and Wales. Rod licences are issued by the Environment Agency and cover the use of up to two rods, running from 1st April to 31st March each year (equivalent to one season).

The easiest way to obtain a rod licence is online and relevant information is provided in the help list of this book. You may also purchase a rod licence over the counter at the post office, via telephone or by direct debit.

For those unsure about making a long-term commitment to coarse fishing, licences are also available for one day or eight days, ideal options for the wavering first-time angler. For the season from 2013 to 2014, prices range from £3.75 for one day to £27 for a full season. Concessions are available for seniors over the age of 65 and for all anglers receiving a Disability Living Allowance or for those in possession of a Blue Badge.

Junior licences are available for young anglers between the ages of 12 to 16 at significantly reduced prices (currently £5).

It is illegal to fish without a licence and hefty fines may be imposed on any anglers caught fishing without one. The funds raised through the sale of rod licences are invested in fisheries for the benefit of all anglers.

Experienced anglers wanting to fish with three or four rods require two rod licences.

A note of caution: If you do buy your rod licence online, be aware of service charges which may be levied by some providers. To avoid online service charges when purchasing your rod licence always apply via the post office website. The website address can be found in the help list of this book.

Northern Ireland

Northern Ireland's Department of Culture, Arts and Leisure (DCAL) offers a range of coarse angling rod licences and permits, similar to the Environment Agency in England and Wales.

Some of the salient points to note include:

- Coarse fishing licences run from January to December.
- A juvenile licence is required by anglers aged between 12 to 18 years old.
- A juvenile permit is required for anglers aged 18 and under.
- Concessions are available for people aged 60 or over and for anglers with a disability.

Licences and permits for coarse fishing are available from three days at a cost of £3.50 up to £17 for a full season (January to December).

A concessionary coarse fishing licence for a senior citizen and people with disabilities costs £5 per season.

The cost of a licence for a coarse fishing juvenile season (from the age of 12 up to the holder's 19th birthday) is £2.

Full details of where to find further information are available in the help list.

Scotland

No rod licence is required to fish in Scotland. The Scottish Federation for Coarse Angling is a useful source of information for anglers living in Scotland. Again, details are provided in the help list.

What will I need to get started?

Chapter 2 covers an in-depth breakdown of the equipment and clothing needed to begin your coarse angling career but here we present an overview of the basics.

What will it cost?

Entering the arena of coarse fishing has never been easier. With all types of angling growing in popularity, launching your coarse fishing hobby has also never been cheaper. Most sports require the investment of a considerable sum of money on suitable clothing and equipment before taking part, but in the world of coarse fishing this is unnecessary.

For only a few pounds, you can purchase enough equipment to enable you to catch a variety of small species of fish. If you enjoy your foray into the angling world and feel confident enough to expand your horizons, you can spend as little as £20 to £60 for a 'starter' kit. The basic fishing tackle that you will need to get started with your new hobby is:

- A general purpose rod 12 feet long.

- A fixed spool reel and line to put on it.

- An assortment of hooks, weights, floats, leads, and a plastic disgorger to remove hooks from the mouths of the fish you catch.

- You will also need some bait to lure your prey; the most common bait is maggots which are purchased in pints. A pint of maggots is ample for that first trip.

- A rod rest/bank stick to rest the rod on when waiting for bites.

You will probably find your local fishing tackle shop an invaluable source of advice on the most suitable equipment for a novice. Many of them are owned and run by ardent anglers always happy to offer guidance on the most productive place for your debut fishing trip (i.e. the easiest place to catch some fish!)

Some fishing tackle shops also sell a range of DVDs and books aimed at the beginner. Quite a few have free catalogues and videos which can help the budding angler. Look out for the regular angling press too for sources of tips and useful information, from the local newspaper columns to the monthly glossy magazines and weekly angling papers. All of them offer a wealth of advice for anglers of all levels.

What should I wear?

Dedicated anglers fish in all weathers, from the sublime to the frankly quite ridiculous. Whatever your preference, you should be prepared for the inclement British climate with suitable clothing. At the bare minimum this should comprise several layers to ensure you remain comfortable, sturdy footwear and suitable headgear (that means hats in summer and specialist fishing umbrellas in winter).

Observing basic safety rules

Coarse fishing is an extremely safe sport but all water is potentially dangerous. When looking for a suitable spot to begin your fishing, it is important to keep in mind the following basic guidelines. All of them are common sense but worth highlighting, especially for the inexperienced angler:

- Do not fish either underneath or close to electricity pylons or cables.

- Avoid fishing close to locks and weirs.

- Check out the safety of the riverbanks and the area you choose to fish, especially if it has been raining heavily the day before. Muddy riverbanks can be hazardous.

- Always let someone know exactly where you are going and what time you will be home.

'You will probably find your local fishing tackle shop an invaluable source of advice.'

What are permits and day tickets?

The majority of freshwater fishing in the UK requires a permit from the landowner or the angling club which looks after the water. Like rod licences, on some waters it is possible to buy a single day ticket so you are not making a long-term commitment. Some waters will require you to join the local angling club which involves purchasing a season ticket.

All club and individual fisheries have their own set of rules relevant to the water you are fishing on. The details are normally printed on the permit and will relate to the types of fishing you are allowed to carry out, the types of baits you can use and also the times you are allowed to fish. Some waters do not allow night fishing, for example. All waters are supervised, usually by the owner or an appointed committee man, whose role is to ensure that rules are being observed.

Contrary to the traditional image of 'bailiffs', local club bailiffs are normally happy to offer advice to new anglers and will take a genuine interest in the success – or otherwise – of your efforts.

Commercial still water sites and club day ticket waters charge anything from £2 upwards for a single day's fishing. Concessions are normally available for disabled people and young anglers and many fisheries now provide onsite refreshments such as small cafés.

Chapters 7 and 8 provide detailed breakdowns of a day's fishing at a commercial fishery, on a lake and at a river.

Is there a closed season in coarse fishing?

From 14th March to 16th June each year, there is a closed season for coarse fishing in England and Wales which applies to all freshwater rivers and streams. No fishing is permitted during this time as fish may be spawning.

The closed season was abolished in recent years on still waters such as lakes, ponds, reservoirs and canals, although regulations for individual fisheries may vary. Anglers should always check the small print on the permits every year as the rules may be subject to change.

Scotland and Northern Ireland do not have a statutory closed season in place but rules and regulations may vary at individual fisheries and loughs. As a general rule of thumb, check with your chosen destination beforehand rather than turning up unannounced.

Some basic guidelines

Planning your first coarse fishing trip is very exciting but what happens when you catch your first fish? How do you handle it without causing harm? What happens to the hooks and where do you keep your catch until you finish your session? For novices, while thrilling, the first catch can seem quite overwhelming.

If possible, we recommend attempting your first venture into the world of coarse fishing in the company of a more experienced angler. Failing that, as you will soon discover, fishing is an extremely sociable sport. If you head out to a popular spot, you will find that seasoned anglers will only be too happy to help a beginner with his or her first catch.

In the meantime, adhering closely to the following basic guidelines should help to diminish first-time nerves:

'Fishing is an extremely sociable sport.'

- Do not handle your fish with dry hands. Your hands should always be wet to protect the fish from potentially harmful bacteria. Fish are protected by 'slime layers' giving them that greasy feel and it is important to maintain that protection. Carry a towel to clean your hands *not* to hold the fish with.

- Be confident and assertive while handling fish but take your time to avoid any harm coming to them.

- Keep your fish close to the ground and avoid placing them on a dry riverbank.

- The use of barbless hooks will ease the process of unhooking. Do not ever attempt to pull a hook out of a fish's mouth, instead use a device referred to as a 'disgorger'.

- Always use a landing net for anything other than very small fish, which should be close to hand before you begin fishing.

If you hold the fish in a keepnet until the end of your session, release them by allowing them to gather at the front of the net. Don't shake them out of the net itself as it may potentially harm the fish.

Don't be deterred by some of these guidelines if they sound complicated at this stage. This chapter is intended as a brief overview only.

What are the golden rules of coarse fishing?

While spending hours on the riverbank, anglers learn to appreciate the beauty of the natural life around them and are drawn to protect it. As well as the environment, it is also important to protect the wildlife too. Below is a brief summary of some of the golden rules to observe while fishing:

- Do not, under any circumstances, litter the area in which you are fishing, always take litter home. Discarded fishing line should also always be disposed of at home. It causes a hazard to wildlife if left on the bank.

- Choosing the right swim for your fishing is important. Stay away from excessive vegetation or obvious obstructions in the water such as tree branches. Be alert for nesting birds; if you do see any make every effort not to disturb them.

- Try to avoid lakes and other popular places where visitors habitually feed the ducks, swans and birds. They will expect you to do the same and may become entangled in your line.

- Do not leave your rods unattended. It is illegal to do so and small animals and birds may attempt to eat bait on hooks or become caught in the fishing line. It is essential to remain close to your rods. If you do have to leave them, remove your bait from the hooks and secure the hooks to the rods.

- Always check your fishing line on a regular basis and especially after each fishing trip in case of any damage caused by wear and tear. Your reel line should be replaced each season or sooner if wear and tear becomes apparent.

- Do not disturb, or cause a nuisance to, other people in your vicinity. Be

'Be proud to be an angler. They are the guardians of our waterways.'

proud to be an angler. They are the guardians of our waterways, as all anglers look out for the wildlife and report cases of pollution, vandalism, etc. to the relevant authorities.

Summing Up

- Coarse fishing refers only to fishing for non-migratory freshwater fish, found in rivers, canals and still waters. It does not include sea fishing or fishing for game fish.

- Numerous health benefits are derived from taking coarse fishing up as a regular pastime. Most notably these include improvements to self-esteem, physical and mental health.

- Getting started in coarse fishing is straight forward and inexpensive. With an initial expenditure of up to around £60 you can begin to explore your potential new hobby.

- Everyone over the age of 12 living in England, Wales and Northern Ireland is legally required to purchase a rod licence to fish. No licence is required in Scotland. Concessions are available for young anglers, senior citizens and disabled people.

- Most waters will require a season ticket or a permit to fish. Always check before setting out.

- Fish should be handled with care and never with dry hands.

- The aim of all anglers is to protect and preserve the natural environment, including its wildlife. Observe the golden rules of angling to ensure minimum disruption to birds and small animals.

- Fishing is not allowed on the rivers from March 14th to June 16th inclusive in England and Wales. Scotland and Northern Ireland do not have official closed seasons

- Coarse fishing is fun, relaxing and the most popular participant sport in the United Kingdom.

Chapter Two

Getting Started

As we hinted in chapter 1, devoted anglers will fish in any kind of environment or weather conditions, regardless of how extreme they may be. From howling gales and freezing fog to the soaring temperatures of a sun-baked summer day, as an angler you have to prepare for every eventuality. Take a walk along any river in the depths of winter on an early morning and you will at some point encounter a solitary angler focused solely on the task in hand.

While we have touched on the basic requirements for your initial venture into coarse fishing, in this chapter we detail the type of clothing and equipment needed as a beginner, come rain or shine.

What should you wear for a day of coarse fishing?

Most experienced anglers possess two separate sets of clothing, one for spring/summer and one for autumn/winter. British summertime in particular is notoriously unpredictable. Even in the height of summer there will be days where you will feel cold while sitting still for prolonged periods on a riverbank or on a lake, especially when the sun suddenly disappears behind the clouds.

Depending on the time of year and the weather forecast, consider the following:

Trousers

Always wear trousers rather than shorts. The sometimes cleverly disguised clumps of nettles and thistles along the riverbank can grow to quite a height and catch you off-guard. Beginning the day soothing unexpected stings may

'Most experienced anglers possess two separate sets of clothing, one for spring/ summer and one for autumn/ winter.'

distract you from your fishing. Leave quality, fashionable clothes at home as you are likely to return with pulled threads and the occasional tear. Choose some rugged trousers that can withstand an encounter with anything possessing spikes or stings. You'll be grateful that you did.

Jackets

For most of the year you will generally require a waterproof jacket for your angling excursions. A useful tip for the summer is the purchase of a coat or jacket with a detachable hood. When a promising summer's day is spoilt by a sudden downpour you'll be extremely thankful.

Hats

As your parents probably told you as you were growing up – and possibly still do – most of your bodily heat escapes through your head. A hat is essential for every angler all year round. In winter, your typical 'beanie' hat is sufficient to keep the warmth in. For the summer months, opt for a hat with a brim to protect your face and eyes from the glaring effects of bright sunshine reflected off the surface of the water.

Footwear

Sturdy walking boots are essential for anglers who generally spend a lot of time walking up and down uneven riverbanks. Ideally, a solid pair of lace-up boots will provide the most support and protection for your feet. The only exception is if you are spending time standing in the water where a supportive pair of wellingtons or waders is vital. For beginners who are still familiarising themselves with everything needed to get started with their new coarse fishing hobby, we don't recommend spending long periods in the water so boots will suffice.

Layers

Always be prepared for a drastic change in the weather and check the forecast before you go out. Even on a hot summer day take several layers, such as a heavy shirt or a fleece for later on in the day when the temperature may drop. For unexpectedly rainy days, a pair of waterproof trousers with an elasticated waist to slip on over your clothing is invaluable; these can be purchased either padded or unpadded. Anglers often need to be waterproof from top to toe and again, you won't regret the effort when you're standing at the water's edge, battling with a stubborn fish.

> **Archie's tip**
>
> 'The most accurate weather forecast is provided by the Met Office's website which gives a forecast by the hour and is updated regularly. While no weather forecast is foolproof it's the one I rely on when the weather forecast is uncertain.'

Accessories

Anglers always require a range of accessories all year round which include:

- Sunglasses – In both winter and summer, sunglasses are an essential accessory. Archie recommends Polaroid sunglasses as they provide that extra protection for your eyes both from the sun and from the reflection on the water's surface. One added advantage is that they may also allow you to see the fish by deflecting the surface glare.

- Suncream and insect repellent – Both are essential during summer, even for hardy anglers (although we're sure some may dispute that). On riverbanks and lakes midges and mosquitoes can occasionally be problematic, particularly at dusk.

- Gloves – Generally gloves are only needed during late autumn and the winter months. Fingerless gloves are recommended for anglers who need to constantly handle a variety of baits. Thick woollen gloves will inhibit your ability to set up your fishing rod and tackle properly.

- Refreshments – These are always essential for a long day's fishing. Take flasks of warm drinks as well as cold drinks to stay hydrated. If your intention is to spend all day fishing, don't forget your packed lunch and snacks. You'll be surprised at how luxurious a steaming cup of coffee will be on a freezing riverbank in the depths of winter.

Avoiding the winter blues

Subzero temperatures are frequently seen in the winter months, even during the daytime. Stay warm by wearing thermal clothing such as long johns, multiple layers of warm clothing, bulky sweaters and jumpers. The padded version of the waterproof trousers mentioned previously will also prove to be a treasured purchase.

'Traditional army stores and specialist "outdoor pursuits" shops offer a wide range of clothing which is ideal for fishing.'

Where can I find suitable clothing?

If your budget allows, brand names such as Barber and Gortex provide excellent jackets and clothing suitable for coarse fishing but you do not need to go to great expense to begin your new hobby. Fishing tackle shops also offer a wide range of clothing and accessories and staff will be happy to provide advice. Traditional army stores and specialist 'outdoor pursuits' shops offer a wide range of clothing which is ideal for fishing. Your local town market is also a useful resource for cheap, yet warm clothing. When you begin to look around you'll be surprised at how many outlets provide clothing suitable for anglers.

What basic fishing tackle and equipment will you need to get started?

Now you have the lowdown on what to wear, we will look at the basic tackle you will need to begin what we hope will be a life-long hobby for you. As we mentioned in chapter 1, all of the equipment and tackle needed for a fledgling angler can be sourced cheaply. This avoids a costly outlay for a hobby that you may decide you don't wish to pursue – although we are hoping for the opposite outcome.

For your first few coarse fishing 'expeditions' you will need the following basic equipment.

Chair

In the 'old days' anglers would pile everything they needed for a day of fishing into a wicker basket – or 'creel' as it used to be referred to – and use the basket itself to sit on. Today's angler is more sophisticated and will find a range of specialist fishing chairs available. For the casual angler, the inexpensive fold-down chairs that can be purchased from camping shops are sufficient for a day by the water.

Archie's tip

'For serious anglers, your ideal chair is one that comes with four individually adjustable legs, available from good tackle shops. They are best for all occasions, but especially those when you find that your chosen fishing spot comes with an uneven bank'.

Rods

There are an extensive range of rods available for all types of fishing. For a beginner a good dual-purpose rod, perhaps 12 feet long in two sections, is ideal as it provides two separate top halves which fulfil different functions for the angler.

The two different top parts usually comprise a standard tapered section and a quivertip section. We have discussed the quivertip in more depth in chapter 6 onwards, together with legering and feeder fishing. Another possibility is the margin pole which we have also discussed in more detail in chapter 6.

Avanti Magic Carp Wand 10-10 Feeder Rod.

With 10 top pieces this rod will cover all your legering
and feeder fishing at just £20.

> 'For the beginner
> we recommend
> that you use a
> fixed spool reel.'

Reels

All rods need a reel to store the line on to enable the angler to cast and retrieve
the line and end tackle. Different reels are available for different purposes, for
example:

- Centre pin reels
- Multiplier reels
- Closed face reels

For the beginner, however, we recommend that you use a fixed spool reel.

A 'fixed spool reel' offers an adjustable clutch, which is preset to automatically release a line under pressure in the event of a run from a powerful fish. This 'slipping clutch' will help prevent line breakages, but it must be adjusted correctly. Your local tackle dealer will be more than willing to show you the simple settings needed.

Today, the majority of modern reels are supplied with more than one spool. Some suppliers, such as Dragon Carp Direct/Used Tackle, offer reels that have as many as 8 to 10 spools or more. Extra spools provide different strengths of line, covering perhaps 2lb to 10lb breaking strain. The angler selects the line needed to cope with the fish he is seeking. We provide more detail on this in chapter 6 onwards

For the beginner, two different breaking strains of line may well be sufficient.

Your local fishing tackle shop or online supplier will be able to offer advice on the best type of fixed spool reel and will also be willing to demonstrate its functions. In addition, YouTube offers a variety of videos providing practical guidance on how to set up your basic equipment.

Avanti 8-8 Method Match Reel

A fixed spool reel with no less than 8 spools, an extremely cost-effective option for the beginner at £20.

Landing net

A landing net is a loose net with a long handle, normally on a triangular frame which is used for lifting your hooked fish out of the water. It is an essential item for all anglers.

Barbus Landing Net

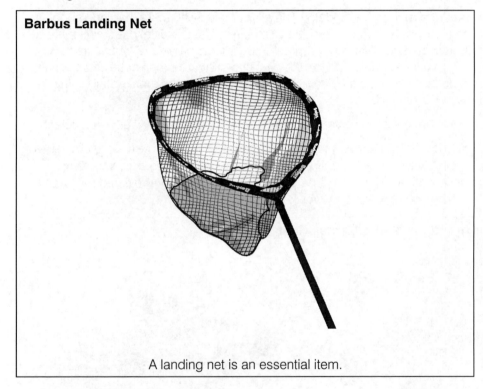

A landing net is an essential item.

Selection of leads

Leads are used in legering, a style of fishing where the bait lies on the bed of the lake or river. We have covered legering in more detail in chapter 6. The lead holds the bait in place on the bottom while you, as the keen angler, observe the rod top – or quivertip – until a bite is indicated.

Hooks

Hooks come in a variety of shapes and sizes and can be bought pre-tied, i.e. a hook with 15 inches of line attached, culminating in a loop at the other end to which the reel line is attached. You can also buy the hooks on their own, usually in packets of 10. Eyed hooks are the ones to choose, but this will mean knots need to be mastered to allow you to attach your own preferred length/ strength of line to the hook.

For the beginner we recommend the use of pre-tied hooks as this makes it much easier to get started in the earlier stages of your coarse fishing hobby.

Details of three basic knots for anglers who have gained some experience are provided in the appendix to this book.

Disgorger

This is a simple device used to remove the hook from the fish's mouth and is available cheaply in any fishing tackle shop.

Floats

Floats come in numerous types but for the purposes of this book we will focus on just two – the waggler float which is fastened at the bottom end of the float only via a metal loop, and the stick float which is fastened at both ends by silicon bands.

Rather than devote half of this book to floats and rigs we recommend you go online and enter firstly 'coarse fishing floats' and secondly 'coarse fishing float rigs' into your search engine under 'Images'. The extensive choice of photos and diagrams will show you in detail the range of stick and waggler floats available and the set-ups they are used with.

For those without Internet access, most fishing tackle shops will provide you with advice. The magazines and publications detailed in the help list also write regularly on these topics.

Split shot

Split shots are literally shotgun cartridge fillings which have been split open to allow the fishing line to be inserted into them. Once the line is inside they are squeezed shut.

Dedicated shot pliers are available from most tackle shops, but in the old days – and in some cases still today – die-hard anglers used their teeth! Please note, we do not recommend this under any circumstances. Boxes of mixed split shot are widely available in tackle shops and normally contain around half a dozen different sizes.

Weights in the smaller sizes now contain no lead due to legislation passed to protect wildlife. All smaller shot is now manufactured using a lead substitute.

Feeders

A feeder is a cylindrical device, usually plastic or metal carrying a substantial lead weight that runs on the main line and is stopped just above the loop of the hooklink by a split shot or other device such as a leger stop. The cylinders (feeders) are used to attract fish by filling them with food items like hemp and groundbait. They come in a variety of styles but for the beginner, we recommend two basic types of feeder:

- Block end
- Open end

Block ends are generally used with maggots, which are easily able to escape through the feeders' holes and hopefully attract passing fish.

Open ends are usually filled with inert material such as hemp seed, sweetcorn, etc. held in place by plugs of groundbait at each end. More information on the use of feeders and groundbait is provided in chapter 6.

Feeders can be easily lost when fishing on the bottom of the water, often catching on snags and rocks. It is therefore advisable to take several with you.

Accessories

When it comes to fishing equipment and tackle, most anglers will find the following accessories useful at some point:

- A penknife or Swiss army knife.

- A small pair of scissors.

- Plasters – especially useful for the inevitable occasions when you manage to stick the hook into your fingers, normally in your excitement at catching an above-average size fish.

Summing Up

- Anglers fish in all types of weather and it is important to be prepared, especially if fishing for a whole day. Dress for the time of year and always take layers for warmth.

- Remember to take drinks and snacks to stay hydrated, especially in warm or humid weather.

- All of the equipment and clothing you will need to get started can be sourced cost-effectively, making your early venture into the coarse fishing arena kind to your budget.

- Use a 'fixed spool reel' for your first full fishing season.

- A landing net is an essential item for all anglers.

- For beginners, it is recommended that you purchase hooks with line pre-attached before you learn the initially complex task of tying your own knots.

- Learning to use block end and open end feeders, plus the waggler float, will give the novice angler a good start to his or her fishing career.

Chapter Three

Fishing Baits Part One – Worms and Maggots

Ask most people what their idea is of what anglers use for fishing bait and they will probably have the traditional stereotypical image of a worm tied on a piece of line attached to a fishing rod hanging over the water!

Today everything has changed. Baits are more varied, sometimes more complex and often require extensive preparation before you set off to your chosen fishing swim. Gone are the days of 'pith and brains', which were quite literally the spinal cord and brains of a bull mashed together and used as bait in the early part of the last century.

For the purposes of this beginner's guide we have divided fishing baits into two chapters. This chapter focuses on the use of maggots and worms as fishing baits. Chapter 4 explains the remaining 'traditional baits', together with an explanation of today's modern baits and what is most appropriate for the beginner.

Choosing the right bait – and understanding how and when to use it – is fundamental to the success and enjoyment of your coarse fishing hobby.

These two chapters are therefore essential reading for all beginners.

'Choosing the right bait – and understanding how and when to use it – is fundamental to the success and enjoyment of your coarse fishing hobby.'

What are traditional baits?

By their very name, traditional baits have been around for decades in the world of the angler. Up to the end of the Second World War, traditional baits included bread, maggots, (often referred to as 'gentles') worms and cheese. Today, maggots and worms remain the most popular baits for coarse fishing.

Worms

The catching and breeding of worms for angling bait can often evolve into a fascinating side hobby for many anglers.

Far from its popular image as a stringy, slimy creature that appears in your garden when it rains, the use of worms for fishing bait has evolved over the decades. Many books and regular blogs describe the breeding and nurturing of worms for bait but here we will only touch on the basics needed for the beginner to get started.

As the good old garden worm, while still useful, is gradually falling out of favour, several more species of worm have emerged as extremely effective angling baits. We have focused on the current popular ones.

Lobworms

Standard baits of the past and present include the extremely large lobworm, often collected by ardent anglers late at night, either during or after a shower. When it rains, the lobworms emerge from the ground, leaving their tails blocking the resulting holes to prevent the water from flooding their living quarters and drowning them.

For keen beginners wanting to source their own lobworms, this is the way to do it:

- You'll need a dim torch, an agile hand, a pile of damp newspapers and a bucket! Wait until after a shower and the worms will be easy to spot, either in your back garden or on local parks, cricket or football pitches – in fact anywhere where the grass is regularly mown.

- Approach the worm quietly and trap it by placing your thumb on top of it to prevent a rapid escape. Any lumbering, heavy footsteps will result in them vanishing quickly back down the hole they've created.

- When placing your thumb on the worm it will contract. As it relaxes you can draw it from the hole. While catching lobworms may prove tricky for your first few attempts, practice makes perfect and many anglers collect large numbers late at night. For best results, don't start until it's fully dark.

Your freshly caught worms can be kept in layers of damp newspaper in a bucket and you will need to feed them until you are ready to use them. Mashed potato is a favourite of most worm species. Place small quantities on top of the damp newspaper, check it regularly, and when it's gone replace it.

Archie's tip

'If you are keeping your worms for any length of time, keep them in a cool dark place out of direct sunlight. A garage floor or anywhere cool is acceptable – heat can be lethal to worms.'

Redworms

Redworms are generally very small, growing no longer than around two and a half inches. Now for the good news; they are inhabitants of manure heaps so if you are intent on unearthing your own redworms, you'll need a pair of disposable gloves, possibly with a peg for your nose!

Like the lobworm, you will need to keep your redworms in a cool, dark place until you are ready to use them but you can keep them in the soil or compost you find them in. Due to the somewhat off-putting aroma we recommend keeping them either outside or in a well-ventilated space.

Brandlings

Another 'old school' breed of worm is the brandling worm, which grows marginally larger than the redworm and is also found in compost heaps. Budding anglers in search of worms will instantly know when they've encountered a brandling worm as it gives off a yellowish, unpleasant smelling liquid when disturbed. While brandling worms were once popular for their ability to attract reasonable numbers of fish, they have been overtaken by the advent in recent years of 'dendys', described overleaf.

Dendrobaena worms

As the garden worm gratefully recedes into retirement, the newcomer taking its place is the dendrobaena worm, affectionately referred to by anglers as 'dendys' for short.

Dendrobaenas feature in some of the earliest angling books you may come across and were once referred to as the 'gilt-tail'. The dendy is a woodland worm which makes its home in rotting leaves. Thankfully, rather than venturing into the depths of the woodland with yet another pair of gloves and set of nosepegs, anglers can purchase their first dendys from a variety of outlets. Either search online for your nearest commercial worm farm or seek advice at your local fishing tackle shop; many sell them in tubs or small bags.

Dendys grow larger than redworms, generally to around three and a half inches and are easily kept in garden compost or peat. Archie has been breeding them for a few years now and shares his experience below:

'For best results with your dendrobaenas, feed them with baked potatoes cooked in the microwave. When the potatoes are cooked break them in half and drop them white side down onto the compost – your dendys will happily feed on the contents. You'll know when the potato needs replacing, when you open the lid of the bucket to find only empty potato skin. Over time you will notice the appearance of round translucent green eggs, which means you are expecting baby dendys.'

With the appropriate care, many anglers successfully breed these worms for several years. They are easily kept in ordinary bucket-sized containers, providing the compost material is replaced every six months or so.

Why should so much effort be made with worms?

As many experienced anglers will tell you, there are several reasons why worms are worth all the effort you put in to keeping them:

- Worms are an excellent and consistent fishing bait, ideal for all types of fishing, regardless of weather conditions. For instance, they often attract fish in subzero, seemingly hopeless fishing conditions, at a time when finding worms in the wild is all but impossible. Dendrobaenas can also be more active in cold water, while other species can be close to comatose.

- They are ideal for beginners in the coarse fishing arena. Once you have sourced your first worms and learned how to keep them, they provide a constant supply of bait, free of charge.

- Every species of fish, including predatory fish, much sought after by specialist anglers, will take worms as bait. Perch in particular have a penchant for them and beginners will also find that fish such as tench, carp and bream are also regularly caught on worms.

Maggots

Are maggots widely available?

The ubiquitous maggot is available in virtually every fishing tackle shop in the country. Even in today's metric world, maggots are still sold by the old imperial pint measure, exactly the same as you get in your local pub. Many traditional shops use an actual pint pot to measure out the correct quantities of maggots for the angler.

Maggots are sold in either maize flour or sawdust. Like worms, they need to be kept in a cool, dark place and out of direct sunlight. You may be surprised to learn that they also come in a variety of colours, the most popular being white, red and bronze.

The adventurous angler may also want to sample 'disco maggots', (don't worry they don't dance!) so-called as they are supplied in every colour imaginable – even a shade verging on electric blue – and generally come in mixed batches.

Maggots are ideal for catching the smaller species, but don't be surprised if the odd better specimen turns up – everything likes maggots; even the local bird life. For the beginner, a pint of white maggots and around a quarter of a pint of 'discos' for added colour is ideal for a day's fishing.

What is a caster?

When left in their natural environment, maggots – the larva of the common bluebottle fly – will chrysalise and form what is now commonly known as a caster. Until the early 1960s, casters were in fact referred to as 'chrysalis'. Like maggots, tackle shops also sell casters by the pint. They are much more expensive than maggots, however, and a little more difficult to put on the hook.

Casters are favoured by many anglers for their ability to attract a better size of fish of several species. The best fish catchers are light brown casters. To prevent them from turning darker anglers keep them in a maggot box in a couple of inches of water. The darker casters are not popular as they tend to float away when thrown in and once they have turned black the bluebottle is imminent!

Your local tackle dealer will be able to supply you with professionally prepared casters in airtight clear plastic bags. These will need to be kept in the fridge and used within four to five days of purchase

As you will probably have noted, anglers have a tendency to produce unwanted clouds of bluebottles, a variety of unpleasant odours and think it's quite normal to keep worms as pets!

'Casters are favoured by many anglers for their ability to attract a better size of fish of several species.'

Why are dead maggots used as fishing bait?

In the early 1990s, Archie's groundbreaking *Fantastic Feeder Fishing* book took an in-depth look at a 'new' topic, the use of dead maggots in coarse fishing.

Depending on the type of fishing you opt for, which we will explore in chapter 6 onwards, dead maggots can prove to be, at times, a superior bait compared to live maggots.

You can prepare your dead maggots as follows:

- For your first trial with 'deads', put half a pint of live maggots into a plastic freezer bag, squeeze out all of the air, then seal it.

- Place the bag into the freezer for a minimum of 48 hours. Don't be tempted to remove them after just one day, as they are notorious for waking up after only 24 hours of freezer time!

- Your dead maggots are now ready to use at any time for at least for the next six months.

The advantage of using dead maggots over live ones as loose feed is most apparent when you are fishing on soft silty bottoms. In these circumstances, live maggots will often crawl into the silt and disappear, leaving the angler with no 'free' feed to attract fish into his swim.

Archie's tip

'Many anglers will throw their remaining maggots into the water after a day's fishing. Over time the fish become used to finding drowned maggots close to the bank. Therefore, the crafty angler will occasionally bait his hook with a dead maggot and drop the tackle in by the near bank. This can often result in a bonus fish.'

Summing Up

- Today's anglers use both traditional baits, such as worms, maggots, bread and cheese, in addition to a wide variety of more modern baits. With the appropriate advice and experience, novices can use all types of baits with increasing confidence.

- Worms are a universal fishing bait and ideal for beginners. For cost-effective baits, you can catch, keep and breed your own worms, including lobworms, redworms, brandlings and dendrobaenas.

- Dendrobaenas are one of the most effective worms, particularly in cold water and the ability to breed your own ensures a constant supply.

- Your local fishing tackle shop will be able to offer advice on what the best 'worm' waters are in your particular area.

- Maggots are a very popular fishing bait among anglers and purchased in quantities of imperial pints.

- Casters are also a popular bait – but bluebottles aren't!

- Newcomers to coarse fishing can also use dead maggots as an alternative fishing bait. Freeze for a minimum of 48 hours to ensure that they are, in fact, dead.

Chapter Four

Fishing Baits Part Two – Traditional and Modern

Traditional and Modern

We referred in chapter 3 to the range of traditional and modern baits available to today's angler. In this chapter, we consider the remaining traditional baits together with more modern baits, including an overview of the most advanced.

What other traditional baits are available?

In addition to worms and maggots, the following baits are readily available and very effective.

Hemp

Hemp seed has for many years possessed seemingly magical properties to attract fish such as roach, barbel, tench, carp and so on. Historically, hemp has been occasionally referred to as the 'demon seed' and at times has been banned from use on some waters because of its supposed affiliation with cannabis. Those worried about getting 'spaced out', however, *won't* be able to do it with hemp seed so concerned parents of young anglers in particular have nothing to worry about.

How is hemp used in coarse fishing?

Today, hemp is deemed acceptable as a fishing bait, proven to attract a range of fish, but is perhaps at its best as an 'attractor' feed rather than a hook bait. It can, of course, be used as a hook bait with a small hook, but bites can be lightning fast and many are missed.

Most tackle shops sell cooked hemp either in one pint measures in plastic bags, or in tins. It is, however, an expensive way of using hemp on a regular basis and many anglers prefer to prepare their own. Most seed retailers sell hemp and at the time of writing a 40lb bag of hemp can be purchased for £25-30.

For best results, prepare your hemp as follows (and be warned, the hemp emits what I can only refer to from childhood experience as a distinctly pungent smell. You may want to leave a window open while it cooks):

'Hemp is proven to attract a range of fish, but is perhaps at its best as an 'attractor' feed rather than a hook bait.'

- Place the hemp in a saucepan and cover it entirely with water, leaving it to soak for a minimum of 24 hours. It is important to ensure the water is regularly topped up as it will quickly become absorbed by the hemp.

- After it has been allowed to soak for the required time, it is now ready to be cooked. Bring the water to the boil and allow it to simmer until the seeds start to split, revealing the white kernel inside. As a rough guide, this may take up to half an hour.

- When you see the white internal kernel showing the hemp is ready, allow it to cool in the water it was cooked in. Once cooled, drain off the water and it is ready for use. You can either take it fishing with you that same day or freeze it in plastic bags for future use.

- As an alternative – and to avoid the aroma of simmering hemp wafting through the house – follow the instructions above for soaking the hemp, but use a pressure cooker if you have one. This cuts down on both the cooking time and the smell.

- For added attraction – from the fish's point of view hopefully – flavourings can be added either prior to the cooking stage, or after the hemp has cooled down completely. We discuss the adding of flavours to baits in chapter 9.

Wheat

A real golden oldie bait, today wheat is hardly ever used. 'Stewed wheat', as it was known, can be easily prepared in a flask as follows:

- Fill the flask with dry wheat to about two inches from the top, to allow it to swell as it absorbs water.

- Cover the wheat with boiling water and leave overnight. The dry grains will have expanded to almost 'pea' size and it is now ready for use after the water has been drained off.

Wheat is a very cheap but highly effective bait, particularly for roach and bream.

Bread

Bread is a traditional angling bait generally used in three basic forms:

- Bread flake – No preparation is needed for bread flake. For your day's fishing, simply take a few slices from a thick sliced loaf and place in a plastic bag to prevent it drying out. Pinch out a small piece, squeeze it onto your hook and you are ready to cast. It can be difficult to get it right, but it is worth persevering as yet again this is a cheap but very effective bait.

- Bread paste – This is much easier to use as you can create your own bread paste at home by simply adding water to your bread slices and kneading them into a stiff paste that is firm enough to stay on your hook while casting. This appeals to most fish that feed on the bottom.

> **Note**
>
> When we refer to 'on' or 'off' bottom, this is a term used to describe fishing with the bait on or off the bottom of the river or still water bed.

- Bread crust – This is generally used for fishing on the surface of the water as it naturally floats. It can also be used close to the river or lake bed, held down with a strategically placed split shot. Bread crust is an excellent bait for roach, chub and other fish, but particularly for surface feeding carp.

- Liquidised bread – This is a relatively modern addition to the use of bread in fishing. It can be prepared either with or without the crusts. Place the bread in a blender and spin until it resembles a fluffy mix. For best results, use slightly stale bread. When fishing, a handful of liquidised bread can be squeezed and thrown into the water to attract fish to your swim. The rate at which it sinks or disperses depends on how hard you squeeze your bread.

- Loose feeding with liquidised bread, combined with paste or flake on the hook, can be a very successful method of fishing which will increase your chances of a catch.

Cheese and cheese paste

Cheese is another stereotypical golden oldie of the coarse fishing world. It is usually squeezed gently over the hook until it covers it.

Some varieties of cheese will be too crumbly or soft to use, so it is worth spending some time creating your own cheese paste. Simply mix your chosen cheese and the aforementioned liquidised bread by hand. The aim is to produce a firm ball of paste as discussed in the previous section on bread paste. The more 'aromatic' cheeses such as Danish Blue or Stilton are especially effective for attracting fish with their pungent smell.

> **Archie's tip**
>
> 'Back in the 1970s, when I did a lot of cheese fishing, my favourite bait was Kraft Cheese Slices, as they moulded easily onto the hook. It may be worth beginners trying this out as an alternative to cheese paste.'

What are modern baits?

In the 1960s and 1970s, 'new' baits started to appear in the coarse angling arena, the two principal ones being sweetcorn and luncheon meat, often commonly referred to as 'spam'. These two baits remain popular staples for the regular angler, and can be used in several inventive ways.

Sweetcorn

Sweetcorn is popular among anglers for its ease of use. Tinned sweetcorn – whether it is a supermarket's own brand or designer brands such as the 'Jolly Green Giant' – can be used directly from the tin. If you don't use all the sweetcorn on your day out, the remainder can be frozen.

The one slight disadvantage of using frozen sweetcorn is that the freezing process softens it slightly. This means that when it comes to longer casts it is likely to fly off your hook. If you are using frozen corn, it is better suited to short-range fishing.

Sweetcorn can be either coloured or flavoured. Bait flavouring is an advanced angling topic and more details can be found in chapter 9. While you won't find tins of coloured corn in the local supermarket, your local tackle shop will usually have a supply of coloured and/or flavoured corn available.

Sweetcorn can be used straight from the tin with the remainder stored in the fridge for up to a week, or frozen for future use. Coloured/flavoured sweetcorn is attractive to almost all non-predatory fish.

Advances in angling over recent years have seen the introduction of rubber and plastic copies of sweetcorn which have been used successfully to catch a variety of fish. Artificial baits are covered later in this chapter and also in chapter 10.

'Luncheon meat has stood the test of time and is still regularly used as fishing bait today.'

Luncheon meat

By 1970, luncheon meat had emerged as a highly effective bait, particularly for bigger fish. It has stood the test of time and is still regularly used as fishing bait today.

Like sweetcorn, luncheon meat is available from your local supermarket and can be used straight from the tin. Some varieties come coated in a layer of jelly and fat which needs to be scraped off before cutting the meat into bait-sized chunks. The reason for this is that the high fat content will result in the luncheon meat floating – and it can be particularly galling to watch your hard-earned money drifting away.

You can use luncheon meat at any size from big chunks down to tiny cubes and special meat cutters can be purchased which will help you to chop it into uniform pieces. These can be used both as hookbaits and loose feed.

> **Archie's tip**
>
> 'I have discovered over the years that using luncheon meat as it starts to soften after repeated freezing/defrosting can prove especially attractive to fish.'

Maize

Maize is a very useful bait for bigger fish such as carp, as it is sufficiently hard in texture to resist the attentions of small fish. Due to its hardness it requires drilling and hair-rigging so it is perhaps best left until the angler is a little more experienced. Some tackle shops sell ready-prepared maize in tins.

Boilies

The boilie is a complex yet carefully blended paste, rolled into bait-sized balls which are then boiled until they are hard enough to deter the attention of smaller fish and remain available for the bigger species.

Boilies come in an array of colours, flavours and sizes and are sold in the majority of fishing tackle shops. They are generally produced in 2lb bags and fished on hair-rigs, making them best suited for the more experienced angler. We refer to the use of hair-rigs in the appendix.

The use of boilies as bait has two distinct advantages:

- Their blanket use by carp anglers (the nation's favourite fish) means that other species living in carp lakes learn to eat them on a regular basis. Increasingly boilies are becoming a major bait for many other species.

- They can be left in the water for a considerable length of time in comparison to traditional baits such as bread, cheese and so on. As each location varies, we recommend that you consult your local tackle shop to discover which type of boilie currently works best in your area.

Pellets

As Archie observes: 'Undoubtedly the biggest impact on coarse fishing in recent times has been the use of custom-made pellets which have revolutionised the way we fish.'

Pellets are basically compressed meals, such as fish meal, provided by the fish farming industry. Pellets come in two forms as follows:

- Hard pellets – These need to be fished on a hair-rig (referred to in chapter 10) as they are too hard for the hook. The hair is a piece of line extending below the hook which for pellet fishing often culminates in a stretchy silicon ring into which the pellet is pushed. These rings are known as bait bands. Hooklinks complete with hair and bait bands are available commercially and for beginners we recommend purchasing these ready-made bait band rigs. Instructions for use are provided on the packaging. Again, your local tackle shop will advise you on what pellets work best in your area.

- Soft pellets – These are generally known as 'jelly pellets' due to their rubbery texture. They are much simpler for beginners to use as they are easy to place directly onto the hook. Soft pellets come in a variety of flavours and sizes.

What are artificial baits?

Artificial baits are rubber and plastic copies of a number of popular baits, which have been proved instantly successful in catching fish and – for that reason – are popular among anglers.

'Artificial baits are rubber and plastic copies of a number of popular baits, which have been proved instantly successful in catching fish.'

The most popular 'copy' baits are artificial sweetcorn and maggots which can be purchased in an array of different colours. Copy baits possess all the attributes to catch the species that the real baits do.

Both rubber and plastic copies are proven to be extremely successful in coarse fishing. One of the main reasons for this is that no matter how clumsy the cast, or how many tiny fish attempt to take the bait, the artificial bait remains on the hook or hair until taken by a 'proper' fish. This gives any angler tremendous confidence.

Many other artificial baits are available but they are perhaps better left until the angler has more experience of techniques like hair-rigging.

Miscellaneous specialist baits

Angling techniques are continually evolving and while we have attempted to incorporate as wide a variety of baits as possible for the beginner within this book, the list is seemingly endless.

As you become more involved in your coarse fishing hobby, it will be worth researching the following bait options as you begin to learn what works and what doesn't on your local waters. Examples of these other baits include:

- Floating dog biscuits, especially useful for carp fishing, particularly 'Chum' mixers (yes the dog food variety!)

- Various specialist pastes available from tackle shops.

- Seafood-based baits such as cockles, mussels, shrimps and prawns which are all available from your local supermarket shelves or fish counter.

Many experienced anglers like Archie experiment regularly with baits to see if they can tap into a new attractor, who comments, 'I get a great deal of satisfaction from concocting a new bait, and then catching a big fish on it.'

Summing Up

- Bread is a popular and cheap bait. It is used in four common forms, flake, crust, paste and liquidised.

- Strong soft cheese and liquidised bread make a great combination when mixed into a paste.

- Sweetcorn and luncheon meat can both be purchased cheaply from supermarkets and used straight from the tin, or frozen for use at a later date.

- Boilies are an increasingly popular bait, usually fished on a hair-rig. Various sizes and flavours are readily available in tackle shops. Originally formulated for carp, now many other species are regularly caught when using them.

- Pellets come in numerous shapes and sizes, with soft and hard versions available. If you are unsure of which types to use – or how to use them – your local tackle shop will provide information and advice.

- Many baits are now available in artificial form, but for ease of use sweetcorn and maggots are perhaps best for the novice angler.

- Pet shop stores and supermarkets can provide a wealth of baits for the enterprising angler to try out.

Chapter Five

The Different Species of Fish

Once you have a basic knowledge of the baits and equipment required for coarse fishing, you will need to recognise the diverse types of fish you may catch. In this chapter you will find descriptions of the common, and some of the not-so-common, species found in UK waters.

Small fish

Sticklebacks

Taking their names from the spines on their backs, sticklebacks do not grow bigger than 2 inches in size and are found in slow-flowing water such as canals and some lakes. They are not an angler's fish of choice but you may occasionally catch one while fishing with maggots and small worms.

Minnows

Some of you may be familiar with minnows if you spent time in shallow water with fishing nets as children. Found in the flowing water of rivers, minnows are small fish, reaching only 2.5 inches in size at best. On some rivers, such as the Dove in Derbyshire, they are present in huge numbers. In this case, fishing with baits such as maggots becomes a waste of time, as a minnow will take the bait within minutes of the angler casting in. They can, however, prove useful as live bait for predatory fish such as perch. Minnows are vulnerable to variations in water quality and are among the first species to disappear if the water becomes polluted.

Stone loach

Sometimes known as 'stone rooters' the stone loach spends a lot of time hiding under stones, hence its name. Anglers won't generally encounter the stone loach due to its preferred habitat of smaller streams and brooks, which are unsuitable for coarse fishing.

Bullhead

'Minnows are among the first species to disappear if the water becomes polluted.'

The name of this fish says it all. With a tapered body coupled with an oversized head and mouth unique among coarse fish, the bullhead is more of an occasional catch. Preferring slow and still water it often only feeds after dark, increasing its elusive reputation. A size of 3 inches is large for this particular species.

What species of small fish will you catch while fishing?

As a beginner, you may notice a few of the following fish species cropping up on a regular basis:

Ruffe

The ruffe is a member of the perch family, shown by its spiky back fin. Reaching no more than 3 or 4oz in weight, it is not widely found in the United Kingdom. However, when anglers do encounter ruffe it is normally present in good numbers, preferring slow water habitats such as the Trent-Mersey canal, among others. In such locations, ruffe can be caught in large enough numbers to give the keen match angler a winning weight of fish. Worms and maggots are usually successful baits when fishing for ruffe.

Gudgeon

The gudgeon is a popular small fish reaching a size of up to 4 inches long and found in large numbers in the right habitat, preferring rivers and canals rather than still waters. Like the ruffe, it can prove to be a match winner for the competitive angler and will take a variety of baits.

Bleak

This small silver-scaled fish can reach up to 5 inches long on occasion and up to 3oz in weight, although most of the bleak caught by anglers are somewhat smaller. It is mainly a river fish, preferring to feed up in the water or at the surface. Again, large numbers of bleak can be caught in a session from rivers such as the River Wye in Herefordshire. Here they can be taken in such quantity that many fishing matches have been won with them.

Which species do anglers prefer to catch?

While the smaller fish may be a novelty for the beginner, as well as giving an edge to the match angler, the following species of fish are more popular with anglers. For the purposes of this guide, the species are divided into predatory and non-predatory fish.

As a guide for angling newcomer we have included a 'worthy' size and a 'specimen' size to give you something to compare your catches against. Don't be disappointed if your early captures don't measure up; experience will lead you to better catches.

A 'worthy' catch is one that most anglers would be very happy with. A 'specimen' is definitely something to write home about!

Please note, we have not included current British records as these are subject to change. We have, however, provided information of where to find regularly updated records via the fishing publication *Angling Times* in the help list.

Non-predatory fish

The species of non-predatory fish include:

Dace

The natural habitat for dace is rivers, and in the faster shallower reaches it can be found in shoals. Dace can reach over 1lb in weight and for the novice, catching these bars of silver can be a good day out. Maggots can be as good a bait as any for this species and float fishing is the ideal way to catch them.

Worthy: 8oz   **Specimen:** 12oz

Roach

'A session fishing for roach with the stick float on a river is considered by many to be the ultimate angling experience.'

Before the advent of commercial fisheries stocked with large numbers of carp, the roach was generally perceived as the angler's favourite fish. It is found almost anywhere, from lakes, reservoirs, gravel pits and ponds, to rivers, canals and streams. It can be caught on a large variety of baits from maggots to boilies and at all times of the year. It can also be taken at any time of day or night. A session fishing for roach with the stick float on a river is considered by many to be the ultimate angling experience.

Worthy: 1lb   **Specimen:** 2lbs

Rudd

Similar in appearance to the roach, the rudd possesses a more golden hue with vivid red fins. Found in the fens and drains of eastern England, plus a few other localities, the rudd is not at all widespread nationally, and is a prize capture. It feeds mainly up in the water, and waggler fished maggots, or floating crust on the surface, can be successful.

Worthy: 2lbs   **Specimen:** 3lbs

Chub

Traditionally a river fish, the chub has also been introduced into several canals and still waters around the country in recent years. The chub is popular among anglers as it will devour almost anything, from frogs and insects to pellets, boilies and plastic baits. It is tolerant of a wide water temperature range making it an excellent winter target when other fish are reluctant to feed due to the cold. In spite of its unfussy eating habits, the chub is an extremely cautious fish, easily spooked by anglers placing their chairs too heavily on the riverbank, or generally thumping about.

Worthy: 4lbs   **Specimen:** 6lbs

Bream

Bream, a true shoal fish.

The bream is a deep-bodied fish found almost everywhere, but its natural habitat is still waters: lakes, pits, reservoirs, etc. They are often nocturnal feeders which means they are more suitable for experienced anglers. The angler who gets up early or stays late into the evening will catch them and may find waters where they feed well in the daytime. Bream will take a variety of baits, with sweetcorn a good starting point. While they are not the best fighters their deep bodies and bronze hue give them a very impressive appearance.

Smaller bream, up to a couple of pounds in weight, are affectionately nicknamed 'skimmers' due to their flat shape.

Worthy: 5lb   **Specimen:** 10lb

Tench

A true fish of warmer weather, the tench is rarely caught in the winter months. A creature of still and slow-flowing water, the preferred habitat of the tench is a weedy lake, as it can forage easily through the densest of weed beds.

Varying in colour between olive-green and brown, the most striking feature of a tench is its red eyes. Another notable feature is its small scales, covered in a heavy mucus coating making the fish very difficult to hold. Putting up a memorable fight when captured, the tench is a very popular sport fish, with dedicated tench fishers' clubs for its keenest followers. Often caught in the early morning, tench will take a wide variety of baits from traditional maggots and worms through to modern plastics.

Worthy: 5lbs   **Specimen:** 8lbs

Barbel

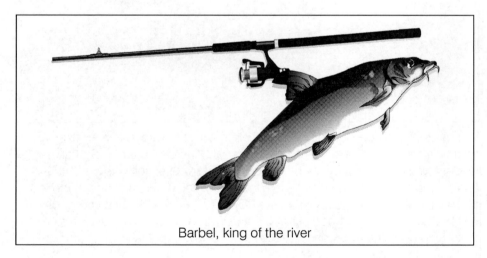

Barbel, king of the river

Known as the 'river king' due to its size and sheer brute strength, this long, streamlined fish is perfectly adapted to fast-flowing water. Of all freshwater fish, the barbel has a particular appeal to anglers and has its own cult following. At least three specialist angling clubs in the UK are devoted to its capture. Today, the barbel is far more widespread than in years gone by, thanks to a successful breeding policy adopted by the Environment Agency's Calverton Fish Farm in Nottinghamshire. Barbel will take all the regular baits, including plastics.

Archie's tip

'Don't go barbel fishing without hemp. Two pints of this, with perhaps a few small pellets added, deposited on the bed of the river can attract any barbel in the area.'

Worthy: 7lbs   **Specimen:** 10lbs

Carp

In the 1960s, the carp was a rare species and considered difficult to catch. In the past few years all that has changed, with the advent of commercial fisheries. A farmer can quite literally dig a hole in the ground, fill it with water, then stock it with carp bought from the various fish farms around the country that specialise in the breeding and selling of carp.

Such waters are known as 'commercials' and charge from £5 upwards for a day's fishing. We mentioned these briefly in chapter 1 and will discuss a day's fishing at a commercial fishery in detail in chapter 7. A large number of such fisheries now exist in the UK, making carp fishing available to all anglers. For the beginner they are an excellent starting point, as their heavy stock levels virtually guarantee you will catch, and they'll take almost any bait you offer them.

Worthy: 10lbs   **Specimen:** 20lbs.

'Of all freshwater fish the barbel has a particular appeal to anglers and has its own cult following. At least three specialist angling clubs in the UK are devoted to its capture.'

Grayling

The grayling is not particularly widespread as they prefer the clear fast-flowing upper reaches of the cleanest rivers, and are always the first fish to succumb to water pollution. Due to their willingness to feed in the coldest water, however, they are worth seeking out in winter. Float fished or legered maggots are as good a way as any to catch them. They grayling is a very striking-looking fish with a large and delicately hued dorsal fin and popularly known as the 'Lady of the Stream'.

Predatory fish

A predatory fish does exactly what its description suggests; it preys on other smaller fish – or in the case of pike, sometimes small mammals and even fowl. Here we highlight the popular predatory fish in the UK.

Pike

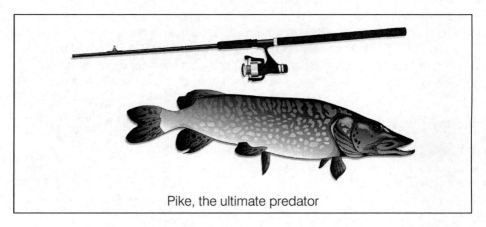

Pike, the ultimate predator

The ultimate predatory fish in British waters is the pike, which can be caught on a variety of live or dead fish and artificial lures. For novice anglers pike are best left alone early in your career as they generally run large and possess an impressive set of teeth. They also require specialist handling when caught.

Worthy: 15lbs   **Specimen:** 20lbs

Zander

The zander is a comparatively new fish in British waters and still a fairly rare catch for most anglers. With their unusual appearance and fearsome teeth, zander are often thought of as a pike/perch hybrid, but they are in fact a unique species in their own right. As with pike, it is recommended that you do not attempt to catch zander until you have more experience.

Worthy: 7lbs   **Specimen:** 10lbs.

Perch

'For novice anglers pike are best left alone early in your career as they generally run large and possess an impressive set of teeth.'

Perch, the underwater bully boys

For junior anglers, and newcomers to coarse fishing, the perch is an ideal predatory fish to pursue. Smaller perch are comparatively easy to catch, especially when using worms as bait. With its red fins, dark stripes and spiky back fin, it is also visually striking. Found in every type of water, perch are especially attracted to worms but can also be caught on maggots, with the larger specimens falling to small live baits and lures.

Worthy: 2lbs   **Specimen:** 3lbs

> **Archie's tip**
>
> 'When winter fishing I've found that the Dendrobaena worm often outfishes the much vaunted lobworm. In fact, out of several hundred fish over 2lbs, I've never had one on a lobworm.'

Eels

As a species, eels are a lot less widespread than they used to be and are currently on the protected list. Small eels are caught irregularly by anglers in a variety of waters and the novice may be surprised to find he/she has only caught a small eel, as they fight like a much larger fish! Big eels are a difficult target for UK anglers and have a specialist group devoted entirely to their capture. Their pursuit is probably best left to the more experienced angler.

Worthy: 3lbs   **Specimen:** 5lbs

What other species of fish are caught in the UK?

In more recent times, several additional species of fish have been introduced, either legally or illegally, into the UK. They are generally encountered at either specialist waters or the numerous commercial fisheries. A very brief summary of these fish follows:

Catfish

Catfish are very powerful fish which can grow to huge sizes (90lbs has been recorded in the UK), and tackling such fish demands specialist equipment. They are not recommended for the beginner.

Sturgeon

While the eggs of the sturgeon are popular in the fine dining industry as caviar, the sturgeon is not common in this country. If caught at all it is often purely coincidental and often by anglers spending a day carp fishing. Sturgeon weighing in excess of 40lbs have been caught in the UK.

Exotics

Exotic species of fish may occasionally be encountered while coarse fishing in the UK, such as the golden orfe, blue orfe, ide, grass carp and fan tailed crucians. Goldfish are also now found in numbers. These are identical to the goldfish you win at the fairground and keep in a bowl at home, but grow much bigger in the wild reaching weights of over 1lb.

F1 carp

No discussion of British coarse fish species would be complete without considering the Frankenstein of the angling world – the F1 carp. This fish has been literally produced to order, by artificially crossbreeding the larger common carp with the much smaller crucian carp. The reasons for this are outlined below:

- Hybrids such as the F1 don't normally breed so commercial fishery owners and fish farms can keep an accurate record of their stocks.

- They are a hardier fish than their parents, and will continue feeding in the cold weather.

- Their growth peaks at around 6lbs or thereabouts, so match anglers can deal with them without risk to expensive rods and poles. The larger carp species have often smashed rods and lines during matches, sometimes resulting in a premature end to an angler's match day.

The F1 has been created to make money and has done so very successfully, being found in the majority of commercial fisheries around the UK.

Summing Up

- An array of fish species are available for the new angler, from the smaller varieties ideal for beginners, to the large predatory fish pursued by specialist anglers, such as pike.

- Popular smaller species include gudgeon, bleak and ruffe. When caught in large numbers these fish often prove to be match winners for anglers taking part in competitions.

- Due to the emergence of numerous commercial fisheries, carp fishing is the ideal place to start for the coarse fishing beginner.

- For the angling newcomer, perch are a relatively easy predatory fish to catch and are found in most types of water. They can be caught with traditional baits such as worms and maggots, as well as live baits and lures.

- The ultimate predatory fish is the pike, which requires specialist handling. Pike fishing is recommended for the more experienced angler.

- Several additional species have been introduced into Britain in recent years including catfish and zander. The common goldfish is also becoming widespread in commercial fisheries.

- The F1 carp has been produced through the artificial crossbreeding of the common carp and crucian carp and is now found in the majority of commercial fisheries.

Chapter Six

Angling Styles

Before we begin to look at how to get the most out of a day's fishing, either on a still water or a river, a basic understanding of the different angling styles is needed. For the purposes of this guide, an 'angling style' is defined as a technique used in coarse fishing. In this chapter we focus on techniques suitable for all anglers, but especially those new to the sport.

As some styles of coarse fishing are difficult to demonstrate accurately in the confines of a book, we recommend that all beginners consult the wide range of online tutorials that are available on sites such as YouTube. Several companies also offer free DVDs.

For those without access to the Internet, the numerous angling magazines will offer guidelines and, as always, observing other anglers is a recommended way to learn effective angling styles.

Again, as we suggested in chapter 2, to save long and complicated descriptions of rigs which would require specialist chapters of their own, we strongly recommend you enter 'coarse fishing rigs' and 'float rigs' into your online search engine, ideally searching under the 'Images' option.

What is casting?

Casting is one of the first techniques learned by anglers. It is the art of using the rod to propel, or cast, the terminal or end tackle – that is the tackle at the end of your fishing line – and baited hook into the water. The best way of learning how to cast properly is by observing other anglers, or asking for help if you find it difficult initially. Your local tackle shop will be happy to advise and YouTube will also provide a range of demonstrations of how to cast.

What is waggler fishing?

The term 'waggler fishing' describes float fishing which is carried out by attaching the float to the line by the bottom end only. Waggler fishing is ideally suited for the novice angler.

To carry out your waggler fishing, you will need:

- An 11 or 12 foot rod
- A waggler float and spares
- A packet of Drennan Grippa stops
- Lead shots
- A selection of hooks to nylon
- A fixed spool reel loaded with 4 or 5lb line

How is the waggler rod set up for use?

The waggler rod is set up for use by the angler as follows:

- Slot the rod joints together, fasten the reel to the rod, and thread the line through the rod rings.
- Slide a Grippa stop, or other commercially bought float stop, onto the line. Thread the line through the eye or ring at the bottom of the float, then add another Grippa stop so that the float is trapped between them.
- The float stops, together with the float, can be moved easily up and down the line if it is wetted first, which is how you adjust the depth that you fish at.
- Move the float and stops further away from the hook to fish deeper – and vice versa.
- Tie the end of the line to the loop on the hooklength, and then add shots until the float sits upright in the water, leaving enough of the float top showing to signal a bite – hopefully by the float going under.
- Always ensure that the hook length is of a lesser breaking strain line than the

reel line. In the event of the hook getting caught on the bottom or the angler hooking a fish too strong for the tackle, only the hook length is lost if the line breaks.

Hook size and line strength are displayed on the packet. The size of hook is usually matched to the size of bait; smaller for maggots, larger for pellets, etc.

Archie's tip

'The hook length can be attached by a very small swivel, with the main line knotted to one eye and the hook length knotted to the other, this helps to prevent possible tangles caused by line twists. Such swivels are readily available at tackle shops.'

What additional tips will help with waggler fishing?

The following additional tips will also prove useful to the novice angler while waggler fishing:

- The type of float used will vary in size depending on whether you want to fish at close range or cast out a long way. We recommend using an insert float. This means that the top part of the float – the insert – is literally plugged into the main body. Various sizes of insert can be experimented with.

A selection of insert wagglers (left) and straight wagglers (right)

'Waggler fishing is very effective, as the bait can be fished at a variety of depths, ranging from just below the surface of the water down to full depth.'

- The inserts also come in various colours so when the light begins to fade, you can swap the colour to one that is more easily seen. Likewise, if the wind is strong, a larger insert may be needed to ensure the float is visible in the water's rippling surface.

Why is waggler fishing an effective angling style?

Waggler fishing is very effective, as the bait can be fished at a variety of depths, ranging from just below the surface of the water down to full depth. Fishing the bait on the bottom usually involves a shot used as an 'anchor' to lay several inches of line, plus the hook and bait on the bottom. Waggler fishing can be carried out on any type of water, flowing or still.

The two diagrams on the following page show fishing both on and off the bottom with a waggler float.

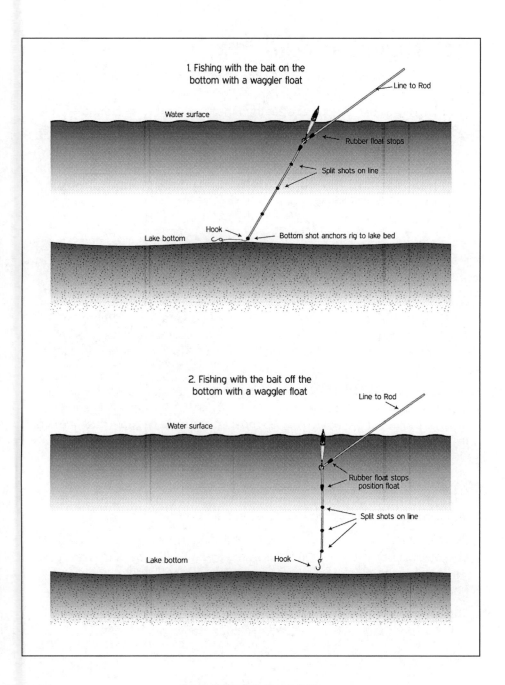

1. Fishing with the bait on the bottom with a waggler float

Line to Rod

Water surface

Rubber float stops

Split shots on line

Hook

Lake bottom

Bottom shot anchors rig to lake bed

2. Fishing with the bait off the bottom with a waggler float

Line to Rod

Water surface

Rubber float stops position float

Split shots on line

Lake bottom

Hook

What is a margin pole?

A margin pole comprises a number of separate pieces of carbon which slot together in a similar manner to that used by chimney sweeps back in Victorian times. Margin poles are much shorter than their more expensive cousins, and are designed specifically for fishing close to the bank, in the water's margins – hence the name.

A pole does not have a reel or running line, as elastic runs through the centre of the top two sections. The line, with its float and hooklength, is attached to the end of the elastic. The number of sections of pole used depends on how far out in the water the angler wishes to fish.

Poles are produced in lengths of up to 50 feet and are often used at this length to place the bait under an overhanging tree on the far bank of a canal for example. This length of pole can be extremely expensive, with a top-of-the-range pole costing £3,000 and sometimes more.

For the beginner wishing to experiment with pole fishing we recommend purchasing a pre-elasticated margin pole. Alternatively, most fishing tackle shops will elasticate them for you. A pole between 18 and 25 feet is ideal for a newcomer.

Specialist pole floats are also available in various sizes to cope with variations in wind power and subsequent water ripple. Again, your local tackle shop will be able to provide more advice on the most appropriate type of float for margin pole fishing.

How is a margin pole used?

When using a margin pole, you will need to note the following:

- Don't cast as you would with an ordinary fishing rod. Instead, the end tackle and baited hook is lowered into the water, and retrieved by 'unshipping', which means removing pole joints until the hooklength can be reached by hand.

- The pole is then 'shipped' out again to place the baited rig back in the water. This involves feeding it out by adding extra sections until you have achieved the length required to place your float back into position. This must be done smoothly or the pole can bounce around, resulting in some quite messy tangles.

- The 'playing' or tiring out of fish with the margin pole is carried out solely by the stretch of the elastic. Sometimes you may need to frantically add extra lengths of pole if the hooked fish is particularly large and decides to race off into the distance. As the fish tires, the angler then steadily unships pole sections, until the fish is brought to the waiting landing net.

What is legering?

Legering refers to the style of fishing practised where the bait is held on the bottom by a weight, known as a leger weight or bomb.

How is leger fishing carried out?

For legering you can use the same rod that you use for waggler fishing but with the following set-up:

- First, slide the leger weight onto the line via the inbuilt swivel. These weights are generally made of a lead substitute. The line from the rod goes through the swivel, allowing the leger to slide freely on the line.

- Next on the line is a small bead; beads are sold by tackle shops in all colours and sizes. The bead rests on a swivel which is tied to the end of the line and prevents the leger sliding any further down.

- The hooklength is generally 12 to 24 inches long and tied to the other end of the swivel. Use the bead as a buffer between the swivel and leger, this helps to prevent possible damage to the knot that secures the swivel.

- In river fishing bites are signalled by propping the rod on a rod-rest with the tip held high and waiting for the tip to vibrate or bend round when a fish takes the bait. In still waters a bobbin or butt indicator is watched for movement. More information is provided on these items in chapter 10.

- Legering is often referred to as 'bomb' fishing.

What are the advantages of leger fishing?

Depending on the wind and the distance required for fishing, a leger of sufficient weight enables even the inexperienced angler to reach much further distances than with a float. It is also the easiest of rigs to cast for the beginner.

What is quivertipping?

Quivertipping involves the use of a different tip section of rod, culminating in a spigot. This spigot takes a selection of different flexible tips, usually around 12-18 inches long, just as the waggler float takes various inserts.

These tips are known as quivertips; three or four are usually supplied with dual section rods. These rods have two top sections, one with a normal taper suitable for use in float fishing and legering, the second with a slimmer taper culminating in the spigot to which the quivertips are attached. These very flexible tips show up bites far better than a normal rod top.

There are several rods on the market that are sold with these two top sections. They are perhaps slightly more expensive but they can do all a beginner needs by using the standard top for float and leger fishing and the quivertip top for more delicate leger fishing plus feeder fishing.

When are feeders used?

When quivertipping, the 'bomb' or leger weight is frequently replaced with a feeder.

As we discussed in chapter 2, a feeder is quite simply a receptacle to hold 'free feed' during the cast. When the feeder settles on the bottom, the contents eventually empty out close to the hook bait, which hopefully draws in the fish. The most suitable for beginners are the 'block end' and 'open end' feeders:

- Block end feeders – The block end is a plastic cylinder full of holes, with lead attached, and a top that clips on and off, making it easy to fill. It is used mainly with live maggots which rapidly evacuate the feeder when it settles. Regular casting can soon build up a bed of attractive bait in your swim.

- Open end feeders – Just as the name suggests, these feeders are 'open ended', with no end caps. They come either in a cylindrical or rectangular shape with many holes, to allow a rapid inflow of water which helps to expel the contents. Open end feeders are filled with a wide variety of baits, including hemp, liquidised bread, wheat, pellets and much more.

Both types of feeders are attached to the line by their inbuilt swivels or other attachment point.

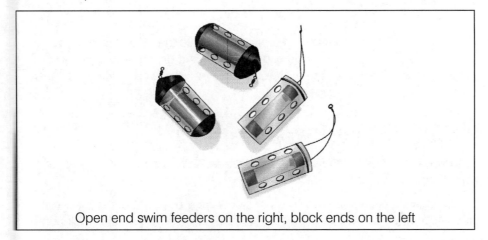

Open end swim feeders on the right, block ends on the left

What else is needed when feeder fishing?

When feeder fishing, a supply of groundbait is necessary to plug each end of your open end feeder. Groundbait is widely available at fishing tackle shops and is normally supplied dry in sealed plastic bags. The groundbait itself consists of a mix of breadcrumbs, biscuit meal, ground pellets and various other meals.

To prepare your groundbait the evening before your day of fishing follow these steps:

- Mix the groundbait with water by hand in a suitable container such as an old washing-up bowl. You are aiming for a consistency just firm enough to 'plug' the ends of your open end feeder, to hold the contents in while casting.

- When the groundbait is damp enough to squeeze into a ball, it is about right.

- At this point tip it into a plastic bait pail and place the lid on firmly. If you are in any doubt about your preparation, mix it on the dry side. You can always add a little more water to the mix to stiffen it up when you reach your chosen fishing destination if needed.

'In coarse fishing terms, the strike is your response to the fish taking your bait, which enables you to hook it.'

What is the best way to strike?

In coarse fishing terms, the strike is your response to the fish taking your bait, which enables you to hook it.

Usually this entails a sharp upwards or sideways movement of the rod which instantly tightens the whole set-up with the objective of driving the hook home.

Over-enthusiasm and a missed bite during your attempted strike may result in the float and end tackle rocketing out of the water at a high rate of knots, often ending up in the nearest tree, bankside reeds, or in a tangle closely resembling a bird's nest.

Don't worry, it happens to all anglers and only experience can teach you to strike in a controlled manner.

The final task is to tire the fish out using the bend of the rod and the slipping clutch on the reel, until it is ready for the landing net.

Small fish can be swung to hand using the rod.

Summing Up

- Casting is a fairly simple technique, generally learned through a combination of practice and watching other anglers. Online tutorials and a range of DVDs are also available.

- 'Waggler' fishing is ideal for beginners

- A margin pole is used primarily for fishing in the margins, i.e. close to the bank. Pre-elasticated margin poles are available quite cheaply.

- Legering is also known as 'bomb' fishing and enables the angler to reach much further distances than with normal float gear.

- Quivertipping is so called as the finer tip used often quivers before pulling round when the bait is taken. When quivertip fishing, block end and open end feeders are recommended for beginners.

- When feeder fishing, you will require a supply of groundbait to 'plug' each end of your open end feeder.

- As with casting, striking is a technique that is learned through practice and experience.

Chapter Seven

A Day Out at a Commercial Fishery

What is a commercial fishery?

A commercial fishery is a lake heavily stocked with fish by the owner, to guarantee visiting anglers will catch.

While the commercial fishery is a still water location, fishing other still water locations such as ponds and lakes requires a slightly different approach. For this reason, we have included a section at the end of this chapter which covers fishing on ponds, lakes, reservoirs and gravel pits.

What can be expected at a commercial fishery?

As we have previously mentioned, developments in recent years have seen the rapid expansion of what are known as commercial fisheries. More and more fisheries appear every year and some now cover areas of up to several acres, with ten or more separate lakes or pools available.

Most commercials are stocked with a variety of fish, although the emphasis is usually on carp.

With more women taking up the sport now than ever before, commercial fisheries now offer a much wider range of facilities. These include the ability to park directly behind your chosen spot (known as a 'peg' and often numbered).

'A commercial fishery is a lake heavily stocked with fish by the owner, to guarantee visiting anglers will catch.'

Some of the larger venues also have specific 'silver fish' lakes or 'big fish' lakes. Most fisheries have built-in platforms at every peg to provide the visiting angler with maximum comfort.

> **Note**
>
> A 'silver fish' lake is a water that isn't dominated by carp, and instead is stocked with a mixture of other species: roach, bream, tench, etc. A 'big fish', or specimen lake is one where most of the smaller fish have been removed. It can be much harder to catch fish at these locations but they are likely to be sizeable, quality fish if you succeed.

Commercial fisheries are, at present, particularly prevalent in England and Wales and also in Northern Ireland. On these waters anglers can either pay on entering or simply turn up and fish on their chosen day. The owner or a representative will come and collect payment shortly after your arrival.

Due to the stocking policies at commercials you are almost guaranteed to catch a number of fish, making them an ideal starting point for the novice. If possible, we recommend you accompany a more experienced angler on your day to help when you encounter the inevitable tangles, or aren't sure about a particular angling technique. Failing that, you will usually find the staff amenable and more than happy to offer advice when requested. Some waters even have a resident 'pro', who can be hired to help you catch, and teach you everything about the fishery.

'It is recommended that you study the rules of each fishery prior to fishing.'

Prices for fishing at commercial fisheries start at around £5 per day. Specialist fisheries, such as those that stock giant carp and catfish, charge up to £40 per day.

What rules and regulations are in place at a commercial fishery?

The rules and regulations vary depending on the policy of the owners. These can include restrictions on the numbers of rods you can use, or the type of fishing which can be carried out at the venue. It is recommended that you study the rules of each fishery prior to fishing. These rules are often displayed on notice boards at the entrance to the fishery.

How do I get started on my first day's fishing?

For your day at a commercial fishery, the following approach is a good starting point:

- Start with either a waggler rod or a quivertip, depending on the weather conditions. In fine weather the waggler offers the ideal way to fish this type of water, as it gives you the option of fishing at a range and a depth of your choosing.

- On a day with little or no wind and especially if the sun is shining, carp in particular will move up in the water to feed. Setting the float at, say, two feet from the hook, which obviously means you are fishing two feet deep, can really attract the fish on such days. The secret of success, however, is to keep a steady trickle of bait falling through the water around the float. This is known in angling circles as 'loose feeding', and this feed is delivered either by hand or catapult. Tackle shops sell a range of different catapults to suit the type of feed being used, i.e. maggots, pellets, groundbait, etc. Whatever you use make sure you keep throwing in more every two or three minutes.

- If the weather is poor, with gusty winds and perhaps rain, use the quivertip rod. On commercial fisheries quivertip anglers prefer to sit sideways on to the water, that is, looking along the bank rather than into the lake. They position their rod on two rod rests, one behind the reel and one about 4 feet in front set at the same height and pointing along the bank rather than out into the lake. The angler sits alongside the rod's handle, waiting for the bite. The baited rig is cast out as normal, and the bite shows very clearly as the quivertip pulls round towards the open water. Without such a right angle between quivertip and lake it would be difficult to spot the bites.

- Either a bomb or feeder can be used as discussed in the last chapter and all the regular baits tried. This includes maggots, bread, corn or luncheon meat; whatever you wish to use on the day.

How is a bite identified on the quivertip?

A bite on the quivertip is signalled by the soft tip pulling round but there are many variations, from delicate nudges to a full-blooded pull round of the tip, which you will need to strike quickly to avoid the rod disappearing into the water!

Sometimes there is a sudden jab round of the tip, then nothing; these are far too fast to react to. Only experience will tell you when to strike, but usually on a commercial fishery you will get many bites, giving you the chance to learn quickly.

> **Archie's tip**
>
> 'In really windy weather, setting the front rod rest lower than the back means that the quivertip will be close to the water's surface. This helps both with observing the tip, and for keeping the rod out of any breeze and as still as possible, improving the angler's chances of detecting the sometimes gentle pulls on the line.'

'Only experience will tell you when to strike, but usually on a commercial fishery you will get many bites, giving you the chance to learn quickly.'

What additional tactics will help to attract the fish?

While fishing with a quivertip or waggler rod out into the lake drop a handful of bait, such as sweetcorn or diced up luncheon meat, close to the water's edge but along the bank a little way from your position. At 20-minute intervals add a little more bait to the same spot. The aim is to draw fish close to the bank and allow them to feed undisturbed for a while.

The crafty angler will have previously set up a float rod and set the float to the correct fishing depth, which in the margins may be as little as two and a half feet. After a couple of hours pick up the float rod and gently lower your bait onto what should be now a 'hot spot' of fish. Often, a carp will take the bait immediately, but as soon as you strike it will charge out of the swim, alarming any other fish in the area and causing them to flee.

In these circumstances land your fish and follow up by using your other rod to fish out into the lake again, while continuing feeding your nearbank spot as before.

If you repeat these tactics throughout the day you are very likely to pick up several bonus fish.

Is a day spent fishing at commercial fisheries affordable?

Even before you set your gear up at a commercial fishery you will probably have spent money on petrol, your day ticket and your bait. To take along all, or just a small selection, of the baits discussed previously will soon see your costs spiralling to £40 or £50 for your day out.

To minimise your expenditure for a hobby which you may well only be trying out, wheat is a cost-effective alternative for your bait.

Stewed wheat, discussed earlier in chapter 4, is among the cheapest of baits available to the angler. It has the added advantage of hardly ever being used as it is considered 'old hat', but you will be offering the fish something that they have never learned to be afraid of.

Remember, you are fishing on a water that is fished virtually every day of the year. Over time most of the fish have been caught on all the regular baits. This does teach them to be cautious.

Once you have your wheat:

▓ Pick a spot a short distance from the bank that you can easily reach with your waggler float (or the leger/bomb rod if it's really windy).

▓ Set the float so the bait fishes on the bottom; use a single grain of wheat on a size 14 hook.

▓ Loose feed steadily with hemp, plus a light scattering of wheat over the top of it. No fish can resist a bed of hemp, even though the small grains tend to get lost in the bottom debris. Carp and other fish will spend a long time searching them out and you can keep fish in your swim all day if you keep the feed going in at regular intervals.

▓ The fish will find those kernels of wheat scattered around and take them confidently because they've never been caught on them before.

- Be patient, it may take a while for the fish to find your offerings, but eventually they will arrive.

In terms of quantity, three pints of hemp and perhaps two pints of wheat (one flask full) should be ample. If you've bought in bulk as previously suggested you'll be surprised at how little your day's bait will cost.

What types of fish are caught at a commercial fishery?

As we previously mentioned, the majority of commercial fisheries stock carp in large quantities, but there are many different varieties of carp. The following list details the species of carp you are likely to catch:

- The fully scaled common carp.

- The large scaled mirror carp.

- The virtually scaleless leather carp.

- Carp, referred to in chapter 5.

- Crucian carp – the smaller variety of carp described in chapter 5, including fan tailed varieties.

- F1 carp – the genetically engineered hybrid of the larger common carp and smaller crucian carp described in chapter 5. This resilient offspring is much more inclined to feed in winter than other species of carp.

- Ghost carp, an ornamental fish generally with a whitish hue.

Other fish which may be caught at commercial fisheries include silverfish such as roach, rudd, bream and tench. A growing number of venues now also stock chub and barbel and perch may also be found quite commonly.

Depending on the stocking policies of the fishery, less common species such as the ide, the golden orfe and the blue orfe may also be caught.

Pike are generally frowned upon due to their predatory tendencies.

Ponds, lakes, gravel pits and reservoirs

Fishing on other still waters, such as ponds, lakes, gravel pits and so on presents more of a challenge for the novice angler as they are not heavily stocked with fish like the commercial fisheries. Success is therefore not guaranteed and sometimes the beginner may return home disappointed.

The advantage of these types of waters, however, is that the fish can grow to much bigger sizes. Bream are a classic example of this, with some reaching well over 10lbs or more, because there are not so many mouths to feed. Tench may also reach sizes unheard of on commercial lakes.

What additional knowledge is needed to fish on these types of still waters?

For an angler still gaining confidence, feeder fishing with maggots can be a good starting point. Virtually all species will take this bait and the feeder can easily be fished at a far greater range than the float. It is still also worth lightly feeding a marginal area and dropping a bait on that area now and again, as suggested for commercial fisheries.

When it comes to casting, the following tips will help you to consistently reach the same spot:

- Pick out a tree or other prominent object on the far bank or horizon to cast towards, so that you will be depositing all the food from the feeder in the same general area.

- Use the reel's line clip. Having cast your rig to a distance you are comfortable with, just hook the line behind the clip on your reel's spool (see photo overleaf) which means that each following cast will be stopped at the same distance.

'Fishing on other still waters, such as ponds, lakes, gravel pits and so on presents more of a challenge for the novice angler.'

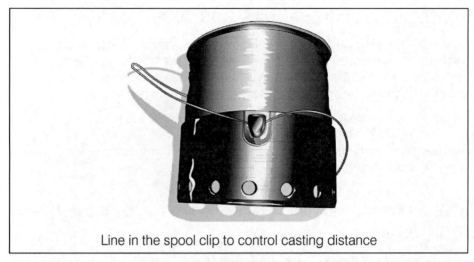

Line in the spool clip to control casting distance

The idea is to create a comparatively small feeding area, in a large expanse of water in the hope of attracting its inhabitants. Of course there is no guarantee that the fish will turn up as they generally will in a heavily-stocked commercial fishery, but if they do you will enjoy a greater sense of achievement at having caught truly wild fish.

Archie's tip

'Due to the much further range you may find yourself fishing at, the catapult will be needed much more. It's a good idea to carry spare elastic, which can be purchased at the time you buy your catapult.'

A keepnet is an optional extra

The keepnet

An additional optional purchase for the days on which you are catching well is the keepnet. Exactly as the name suggests, the keepnet is a net in which you may keep the fish you've caught until you are ready to return them to the water at the end of the day. Your local tackle shop will have a variety of nets to show you.

> **Note**
>
> Commercial fisheries don't usually allow keepnets, other than during competitions.

While the keepnet is by no means essential, many anglers take great pleasure in viewing a good catch of fish at the end of a successful day – and maybe taking a few photos to post on Twitter, Facebook, Instagram or for inclusion in a good old-fashioned photo album, before releasing them back into the water.

Summing Up

- A commercial fishery is the ideal place for the novice angler for their first full day's fishing, as these waters are heavily stocked with fish and a catch is almost guaranteed.

- Use a waggler if the weather is fine, or a quivertip in the event of windy or wet weather.

- For a beginner, recommended baits are sweetcorn and luncheon meat, but maggots are always a good alternative if you are struggling for bites. Wheat is also an excellent cheap bait and effective source of loose feed.

- Commercial fisheries are generally stocked with an abundance of carp but expect to catch fish such as bream, roach and various other silver fish.

- Other types of still waters such as ponds, lakes, gravel pits and reservoirs are best tackled when the angler has gained some experience, as they require slightly different tactics.

- You may want to invest in a keepnet for the days when you catch large numbers of fish to view at the end of your day's fishing. Always check the regulations for commercial fisheries in advance as many do not permit the use of keepnets.

Chapter Eight

A Day Out on a River

When you have mastered your angling styles at the various commercial fisheries and other still waters, you may want to spend time fishing your local river. Here we consider the difference when fishing a river in comparison to a still water, and include detailed insider advice from Archie who explains his 'heavy stick float' method of fishing.

Why is river fishing different compared to fishing on still water?

There are several notable differences detailed as following:

- While the approach to legering and feeder fishing is identical to that described in chapter 7, using the float can be more complex as the water is constantly flowing away from you, taking your float and baited hook with it. What the angler has to do is learn to control this movement, which is known as 'trotting', i.e. trotting the float down the river with the flow.

- If using the waggler the settings can be virtually the same as described for 'off-bottom' waggler fishing in chapter 7. You will have to feed line from the reel, however, so the float and end tackle can travel down the river searching for fish. This is usually done by a light touch of the finger on the front of the reel spool where the line peels off, to keep as straight a line to the float as you can while it moves down the river. Too firm a touch on the spool will cause the waggler to be pulled under, so it's a case of practice makes perfect.

- You may get a lot of false 'bites', as the uneven nature of the riverbed means that the hook and bait may be dragged along the bottom by the current, taking the float underwater. If this happens, inexperienced anglers often believe that they have a bite. To prevent this, slide the float lower, towards the hook and try another 'trot' down the river. If necessary, keep adjusting the float until it runs smoothly through your swim without going under – except of course when you have a bite.

Regular adjustment of the float will give you the option to fish at all depths, whether you want to drag the bait lightly along the riverbed, or present it at different levels.

Note

If you find a smooth weed-free riverbed, you will be able to have the bottom shot and the last few inches of the hooklink, plus the baited hook, actually dragging along the riverbed. This slows the progress of the float down the river slightly. In addition, the drag causes the float to waggle slightly from side to side (hence the term 'waggler').

'Regular adjustment of the float will give you the option to fish at all depths.'

What bait works best when river fishing?

The most popular bait when river fishing is maggots, although in recent times pellets and diced luncheon meat have been used to great effect.

Many other good baits can be used for trotting, for example:

- Sweetcorn and wheat can be excellent on their day.

- Casters, hemp and breadflake can also all be used to great effect, but these three baits are more difficult to use. Casters are easily crushed when putting them on the hook; breadflake comes off the hook at the end of every trot downstream and hemp requires very nimble fingers to attach it correctly to the small hooks normally used.

For the purposes of this guide we will concentrate on maggots. The angler can move on to other baits when she/he feels comfortable with river fishing techniques.

- Talking of small hooks, float fishing maggots on rivers needs fairly delicate tactics; a single maggot on a size 18 or 20 hook, two or three maggots on a size 16 or three or four on a 14. It is rare to go larger than that, other than in specialist angling. Hooklength line strength is generally 2 to 3lb breaking strain, in conjunction with a 4lb mainline. *Always* use a lighter hooklength than the main line. Should you hook a snag on the riverbed or a particularly large fish and suffer a breakage then only the hooklength will be lost.

- As in still water, loose feed is also used to attract the fish but you need to take into account the flow of the river. Throw a small amount of maggots, perhaps as little as 15 or 20, either by hand or catapult into the river slightly upstream of your fishing position, followed immediately with your baited tackle. This should be done every trot down. Some anglers get lazy and stop feeding every cast but this can cause a reduction in the number of bites. River float fishing is a very active business, and many anglers love it for the sheer sense of involvement.

Archie's tip

'In addition to maggots, hemp has proved to be an excellent loose feed for river fishing. It can be fed by hand and thrown in slightly downstream of the angler due to its faster sinking rate.'

Above all, be patient. It may take some time to establish where exactly the fish are in your swim and at what depth they are feeding. When you finally begin to get a few bites, you could finish up with a keepnet full of fish.

Many anglers like to use a keepnet in flowing water as it is kinder to the fish than using one on a lake. The river provides a flow of fresh oxygenated water through the mesh of the net.

What type of fish will I catch on the river?

On bigger rivers like the Trent, Severn, Thames and Wye, you will encounter many different species in one day, typically roach, dace, bleak, perch, chub and sometimes bream or barbel. That popular little fish, the gudgeon, might show, but they are nowhere near as widespread as they used to be.

'River float fishing is a very active business, and many anglers love it for the sheer sense of involvement.'

Are more advanced tactics available?

Several tactics are available to the angler who has some basic knowledge and experience of coarse fishing. Here we focus on stick float fishing and the use of bait droppers, including Archie's exclusive advice on heavy stick float fishing.

What is stick float fishing?

The stick float is one of the harder disciplines of angling to get right but when you do, it is a great way to fish. Follow the guidelines below for the most effective method of using a stick float:

'The stick float is one of the harder disciplines of angling to get right but when you do, it is a great way to fish.'

- You will still be running a baited hook down the river under a float, searching the different depths as you would while waggler fishing. The difference here is that the float is attached 'top and bottom'.

- There are many different types of stick float available, including lignum sticks, wire stemmed sticks and domed sticks, but the easiest type to use is the 'shouldered stick', so called because it has a short brightly painted visible top section with a thicker section immediately below it – hence the name 'shoulder'. This broader section tapers all the way down to the bottom of the stick float, with the extreme end no thicker than the coloured sight tip.

- Attach the float by using small pieces of silicon rubber. These rubbers slide over the float at each end to trap the line in place. The different types of stick float available generally have different diameters. Packets of mixed sizes of silicon rubbers to suit your stick float can be purchased from most tackle shops.

- Sometimes, striking at a bite can cause the float to slip down the line, changing the fishing depth. In such cases the angler may lose contact with the fish. For this reason, a third float rubber is often added halfway down the float to allow for a more secure grip on the line. The top rubber can be set at the bottom of the slim tip, just above the shoulder, which allows the tip to stay above the surface of the water. The angler watches this tip as it travels downstream, hoping it will go under as a fish takes the bait.

- To cater for delicately biting fish, the top float rubber can be moved closer to the end of the tip leaving just a 'pimple' visible. The slightest bite will register but for this tactic to be successful the weather needs to be calm and the angler must have good eyesight.

- As mentioned previously, loose feeding hemp and maggots every cast is necessary – experienced anglers refer to this as 'little and often'.

What are the advantages of using a stick float?

The stick float can be held back against the flow of the river, due to the top rubber, by using your finger lightly on the line where it leaves the spool, to slow it down. (If you attempt to do this with a waggler the float will be pulled under). This means that the hook bait will travel slightly slower than the flow of the current. This tactic will often attract more bites than letting the bait run through at normal current speed.

A note on 'shirt button shotting'

In most magazines and videos you may see the term 'shirt button shotting' referred to. This basically describes the way shots are placed on the line below the float, i.e. evenly spaced down to the hooklength, with the bottom one perhaps around 9 inches from the hook itself, hence the term 'shirt button shotting'. Again, a variety of diagrams showing shirt button shotting for coarse fishing are available online and in the various regular angling publications.

Shots are usually graded in size with the largest nearer to the float and the smallest placed nearer to the hook, and they are graded by numbers. The higher the number, the smaller the shot, for example the highest placed shot may be a No 1, the lower shot could be No 10 or even smaller. Stick floats are similarly graded, 4 x No 4 is a delicate float, 10 x No 4 a heavy one and so on.

Archie's exclusive tip – heavy stick float fishing

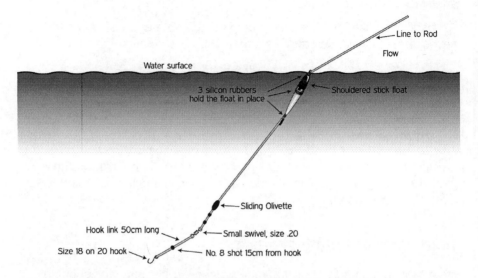

Once you are reasonably adept with stick float fishing you might like to try Archie's version, but beware – other anglers may look aghast at what they consider a drastically heavy set-up! He has, however, been extremely successful with it, so in his own words, this is how he does it.

'In recent years I have developed a rather radical way of stick float fishing and feeding, which is worth covering here as it is far easier to use than the normal stick float rig.

The conventional idea is to use a smaller float and shots to give a delicate bait presentation, in conjunction with the "little and often" loose feeding described previously.

My idea is quite the opposite:

▨ Begin with the largest stick float you can find. At the current time I use a Drennan 7.5bb shouldered stick. Skilled match men would recoil in horror at such a crude approach, but the heavy float rides the water superbly and is almost impervious to bad weather, or adverse winds, which would ruin a delicate presentation.

- The shoulder on such a float is invaluable when 'holding back', as the float does not rise up in the water nearly as much as a lighter float and it is far easier to keep a straight line between float and rod top; this gives the best possible presentation when stick float fishing.

- Rather than a shirt button run of shots down the line, an olivette is used. This is a torpedo-shaped lead weight with protruding ends which have mini pieces of silicon rubber to trap it onto the line, very similar to the way the stick float is attached.

- This is known as the 'bulk weight' and they come in various sizes. Providing you match olivette size to float size, the only additional weight needed is a small shot on the hooklength, perhaps a No 6 about six inches from the hook. The olivette can be moved up and down the line in the same way as the float.

- This gives the angler the ability to position it up near the float, which allows the hookbait to fall steadily through the water searching for off bottom fish. Sliding it down to the hooklength swivel takes the bait down rapidly, defeating the attentions of nuisance bleak which feed much higher in the water.

- The hook length is generally around 18 inches long and can be joined to the main line by a tiny swivel – this swivel acts as the equivalent of a small shot. I will commence fishing in the normal way, running the float down the flow and loose feeding steadily, until I find the point in the swim where most bites are had, from any size or species of fish. At that time I cease loose feeding and reach for the bait dropper.

What is a bait dropper?

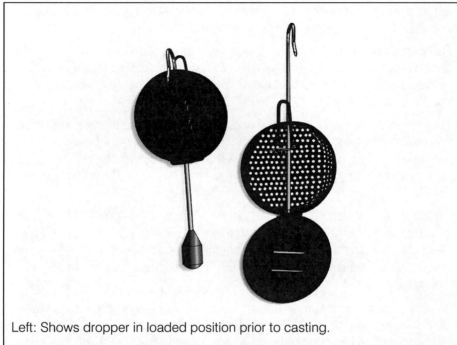

Left: Shows dropper in loaded position prior to casting.

Right: When dropper hits the bottom it triggers the lid to open, releasing the contents.

Similar in function to the feeder, the bait dropper is an ingenious device sold at most tackle shops which is tied to the end of the line, filled with your selected feed, and dropped to the bottom of the river; where it opens to allow the contents to spill out.

Most anglers briefly hook this onto their float tackle (there is a little cork attachment on the bait dropper which you can stick the hook into), to deposit the feed, but I have a cheap old rod, stiff as a poker, which I use solely for the job. I will commence by depositing four droppers each of hemp and maggots on the bottom at my chosen spot. I know now exactly where the food larder is;

the flow of the river is slower at the bottom than at the surface so the bait will stay there a comparatively long time, until it is either eaten by fish or eventually moved along by the current.

The float is then run down to this hot spot and usually a bite can be expected there, and for 12 to 15 feet downstream. When done correctly, the angler can have fish literally queuing up at the spot. You find yourself brimming with confidence, as you know exactly where in your swim the fish will be.

Bites may often come steadily but when there is a notable slowing down don't hesitate to use the bait dropper again, with another four helpings of each bait dropped in.'

What are the advantages of using a bait dropper?

There are two advantages to this method:

- Recent underwater photography has shown that loose fed maggots are often swept right out of the angler's swim before getting anywhere near the bottom. Dropped feed stays within a few feet of its introduction point.

- Several hours of this accurate baiting will not only attract lots of fish to the area, it should eventually pull in bigger species like chub and barbel.

As the day draws to a close, you may opt to swap to heavier leger gear on a separate rod using a larger bait such as a piece of luncheon meat. Hopefully this will result in a real specimen or two before you, the happy and hopefully exhausted angler, head home.

'Several hours of this accurate baiting will not only attract lots of fish to the area, it should eventually pull in bigger species like chub and barbel.'

Summing Up

- Fishing on a river is markedly different to fishing on still water as the water is constantly moving away from you, requiring a change in technique.

- Maggots are an excellent all-round bait for river fishing, while hemp is valuable as loose feed.

- Anglers fishing rivers will need more patience and perseverance in comparison to fishing at a commercial fishery. Sometimes you can spend most of your day searching for bites.

- Fishing with a stick float is a useful technique to learn, although it can take time and practice.

- Fishing with the heavy stick float and bait dropper, once mastered, can bring large quantities of fish including some real specimens.

Chapter Nine

Advanced Angling
Part One

What is advanced angling?

Once you have mastered the basics and explored some of the more in-depth techniques of angling which we have discussed in the previous two chapters, you are ready to progress to more advanced angling.

The rate at which your confidence will increase depends on how often you go coarse fishing and how adept you become with your rigs. Everyone progresses at a different pace depending on the time available for fishing, and how much you enjoy it. The important thing is to move forward with your new hobby at a pace that you are comfortable with, and not to compare yourself with other anglers.

In this chapter we will cover bait flavouring. Many books have been written on the topic of flavoured baits and it is impossible to cover everything here, so again we have focused on the basics.

Thank you to Archie in this particular chapter for allowing me to delve into his *Magic Book on Bait Flavouring*. Many of the bait treatments referred to later on were obtained from that publication. Details of how to purchase the book for those interested in learning more about bait flavouring are available in the book list and help list.

'The rate at which your confidence will increase depends on how often you go coarse fishing and how adept you become with your rigs.'

What is bait flavouring?

In the last twenty years, the flavouring of all types of baits has become almost standard in coarse fishing. Visit any local fishing tackle shop and you will discover a bewildering array of liquids, powders and potions on the shelves, each one claiming to be the most effective. While it may appear to be a minefield to the novice angler, the fact is that even a poor attractor is better than none at all. To help clarify the situation a little, liquid attractors are known as flavours, powders are known as additives.

Why do flavours attract the fish?

Flavours attract fish because you are giving your baits a smell and taste of your choosing. Maggots, for instance, are reared at maggot farms mainly on meat or fish, which of course is not first grade food as this is reserved for human consumption. Your bait is therefore sold to you with perhaps an unappetising smell. By adding flavours you replace that aroma with one that you think will be far more appealing to the fish – and it generally is.

Some anglers don't believe in flavours, but Archie has spent over three decades experimenting and has no doubt that they work 'big time' as he says.

Early tests with the flavours involved fishing side by side with a friend while maggot feeder fishing. One angler fished with flavours and additives, one fished without. The outcome was always the same – flavoured maggots caught more fish every time, with a minimum of five to one advantage.

How are liquid flavours used?

Follow this advice when purchasing your liquid flavours:

- When buying your flavours from your tackle shop, always seek advice about which are currently performing well on local waters.
- After purchasing your bottle (usually 50ml) make sure you buy a syringe or pipette to draw your flavour from the bottle.

- Draw 2ml of flavour into the syringe, expel it onto your maggots then shake them up a little to help disperse the flavour. Do this just before setting off fishing.

- All flavour bottles carry recommended usage levels on their labels, but a general starting point for maggots is about 2ml per pint. Other baits are covered later in this chapter.

As a general rule, spicy and savoury flavours are more effective at attracting fish in autumn and winter, while fruity, sweet-smelling flavours work better during the summer months. Having said that, this is the unpredictable world of coarse fishing we are talking about and on some waters the opposite theory may apply. This is why it it is essential to do your research.

In addition to the advice available at your local tackle shop, a range of online coarse fishing forums also exist, many of these associated with national angling magazines.

How are powder additives used?

Follow the guidance below for your powder additives:

- Powders are used somewhat differently to liquids and in the case of maggots are best added the evening before your day's fishing.

- Two heaped teaspoons full of your chosen powder additive per pint of maggots is about right.

- Spices are excellent fish attractors. Some anglers will quote curry powder to you but bear in mind there are in excess of 600 curry powders worldwide so if you are successful using one make a careful note of its name and make. Your next curry powder might be quite different.

- As far as coarse fishing is concerned effective spices include black pepper, paprika, chilli, coriander, cinnamon, aniseed and turmeric. Several others are available but these are more than enough to begin with.

- The adventurous angler may consider blending two or more together and from there the combinations can become never-ending.

'As far as coarse fishing is concerned effective spices include black pepper, paprika, chilli, coriander, cinnamon, aniseed and turmeric.'

- All of these powders can be added to maggots at a rate of two teaspoons per pint as mentioned earlier.

Archie's tip

'There are literally scores of powders you can use, plenty of them available at tackle shops. In this case you will find a wide choice at your local supermarket, but even better are the specialist Asian shops. The Asian communities have long been importers of every type of spice from around the world and we anglers can be very grateful for that.'

Note

Some of these spices also work as a colour, turmeric being a notable one as it gives baits a yellowish hue. In the same way, chilli reddens baits, paprika turns them pink and so on.

What is the method for boosting other baits?

Here we have featured flavouring methods for specific baits for you to try.

Luncheon meat

- Chop your meat (normally a 300 gram tin) into the size you wish to use. This will depend both on hook size and the type of fish you are hoping to catch.

- Use your syringe to squirt 2 or 3ml of your chosen flavour into a plastic freezer bag, obtained in various sizes from supermarkets.

- Rub the bag beween your hands until the flavour has been smeared all round the inside of it. Drop in your chopped meat, blow into the bag to expand it, then shake it until all the meat has a shiny look where the flavour has adhered to it.

- Now choose your additive and apply 2 heaped teaspoons all over the meat.

- Repeat the blowing and shaking, then let out the air and seal the bag up. Don't forget to add the date, plus the attractor used, to the label on the bag.

- You now have a flavoured meat dusted with powder and ready to go.

- A good example of a flavour and additive to use with luncheon meat would be a pineapple flavour and turmeric powder, but the possibilities are limitless.

Archie's tip

'I strongly recommend freezing your treated meat before use, and will explain why at the end of the bait section on page 101.'

Sweetcorn

- Tip a tin of sweetcorn, complete with juice, into a maggot box.

- Add 3ml of your chosen flavour and stir it in; most fruit flavours blend well with the corn's natural aroma.

- Sweetcorn works very well with the flavour alone so you may choose to leave out the powders on this occasion.

- Take it fishing with you in the maggot box you prepare it in, or bag it and freeze it, as with meat. It will, however, soften a little as it defrosts.

Pastes

If you make your own pastes add a heaped teaspoonful of an additive such as paprika at the mixing stage. Add the liquid flavour to the water you use to start the mixing – a spice flavour would accompany the paprika well.

Today you will find a large amount of 'over-the-counter' pastes on offer in many tackle shops which are already flavoured. If you want to boost the flavour further simply tip the paste out of its container, flatten it down a little and add 1 heaped teaspoon of additive. Mix it well in by hand then flatten it down again before adding 2ml of flavour onto it then mix in as before.

You now have a totally unique bait!

Liquidised bread

In chapter 4 we discussed preparing liquidised bread in a blender which is the time to introduce your additive. In this case the machine does all of the hard work for you, giving you a very different bread feed. You may, if you wish, take it further by 'greasing' a large freezer bag with flavour as mentioned previously for luncheon meat.

Tip in your additive-flavoured crumb, shake well, date and label it and your flavouring is complete.

Archie's tip

'It's a good idea, if you have freezer space, to treat a full loaf, (minus crusts) at one go: for this, use 4 heaped teaspoons of additive and 5ml – a teaspoonful – of flavour.'

Breadflake

For flavouring breadflake, follow these steps:

- Take three thick slices of bread, and prepare a suitably sized freezer bag, ready greased with 3ml of flavour, as described earlier.

- Drop in the slices and rub the bag gently between your hands to transfer the flavour to the bread.

- Take a slice from the front of the 'three pack' to the back, and rub gently again.

- Repeat until all six sides have been in contact with the flavour. Shuffle the cards, so to speak. Date and label it and it's ready for use.

Hemp

As hemp needs to be cooked, it's generally recommended to use only a powder additive as liquid attractors can be virtually destroyed by the boiling process.

Hemp is such a good attractor in its own right that an additive is really all you need, at two heaped teaspoons per pint. Add this to the hemp and water prior to boiling. Allow it to stand for two or three days in the water in which it was cooked and you now have one of the best loose feeds in angling.

Dead maggots

Dead maggots can work so well that sometimes they often outfish live ones – and of course they work even better flavoured.

To prepare them, add the usual 2 teaspoons of additive per pint to the live maggots the day before, to allow them to ingest the powder.

The next day add 2 or 3ml of your liquid flavour, allowing around 20 minutes to ensure it is spread evenly by the moving grubs.

Place the live maggots in a dated and labelled freezer bag, freezing them for a minimum of 48 hours (as we discussed in chapter 3).

When fishing use them as you would use live maggots.

Remember, for feeder fishing with dead maggots you'll need an open ended feeder, plugged with groundbait, as they won't escape from a block end feeder as live maggots would.

Dead maggots will last quite a while frozen, but are best used within three months.

> 'Dead maggots can work so well that sometimes they often outfish live ones – and of course they work even better flavoured.'

Why are baits that have been frozen more effective?

Many baits work better after being frozen and then thawed out for use; here we explain why.

If you've ever purchased a frozen chicken from the supermarket you may have noticed ice crystals inside the plastic bag. This is caused by the moisture in the chicken freezing and being forced out. Really deep freezing can force all the moisture out of meats and other products, hence the term 'freeze drying'.

With our chicken, once it defrosts the liquid is drawn back into the bird.

If we flavour say, luncheon meat, then freeze it, minute amounts of moisture are forced out of it. When we thaw it out these crystals and the flavour mingle and then are drawn back into the bait together, giving it that extra boost.

That is why a flavoured and defrosted bait will often catch more fish than a bait that has never been frozen.

Can I freeze all baits?

If you decide that fishing is going to be your regular hobby, a freezer and a fridge of your own is a good investment. Your family and friends – whether fellow anglers or not – won't always take kindly to finding a tub of wriggling maggots next to the salad! If you scour the local free papers, you can often find good second-hand bargains.

Summing Up

- Bait flavours are fairly commonplace in the world of coarse fishing today. Using flavours vastly improves your ability to attract fish.

- For newcomers to additives, turmeric and curry powder are a good starting point. Add them to baits such as luncheon meat, bread, and pastes.

- When making your own pastes add a heaped teaspoon of additive (powder) at the mixing stage.

- Hemp is an excellent attractor for fish; all you require for flavouring hemp is the additive at 2 heaped teaspoons per pint.

- Flavoured dead maggots are an excellent source of bait.

- When freezing baits, always label the bag with the date, the flavour, or additive used, together with the quantities. If successful, you will want to be able to repeat the experience using the same quantity and type of attractor.

- A flavoured and defrosted bait will often catch more fish than a bait that has been flavoured but not frozen.

- Anglers can experiment with their own powder additives and try out things like custard powder, drinking chocolate, gravy granules and a host of others.

Chapter Ten

Advanced Angling
Part Two

Having introduced you to flavours and additives, in this chapter we consider three elements of advanced angling that will be useful after some experience has been gained.

These are:

- After dark angling – also referred to as night fishing. Fishing in the dark can be very effective as the fish lose a lot of their natural caution.

- Artificial baits – the ever expanding range of artificial baits has brought some huge catches. They have been used on both rivers and still waters to attract a whole range of species.

- Big Fish Rig – a specialist technique which can be used on both rivers and still waters to catch a wide variety of species, from roach to carp.

After dark angling

As you begin to recognise the natural daily rhythms of the coarse fishing world, you will notice that the fish are often far more active at dawn and dusk than during the day. This is especially the case during the summer months. Many anglers prefer to fish after dark at this time of year, looking to catch more, and bigger, fish than they would during daylight hours.

'Fishing in the dark can be very effective as the fish lose a lot of their natural caution.'

What additional equipment is needed for after dark angling?

After dark angling requires additional equipment which you would not typically need for fishing in the daytime. Many dedicated carp anglers, for example, fish not only all through the night but literally through a full weekend. Some spend a week's holiday on the bank, but it is best to start with an 'overnighter'.

Following, we provide information on what you will need.

The 'brolly shelter'

It is vital to keep not only the rain, but the wind at bay, so invest in a brolly with side panels, or a flat back brolly. These are basically large umbrellas with extended sides that sit level with ground. They also have pegging points, metal rings attached at intervals around the bottom edge of the brolly to peg it down firmly. If the pegs aren't supplied they can be purchased separately. With the brolly's centre pole in the ground and half a dozen pegs in place, you're impervious to the weather.

Head torch

The head torch is an essential piece of equipment. If you can afford it buy two, plus spare batteries. If your head torch fails in the night, and you don't have a spare one with you, your fishing trip is over. Tackle shops supply these items, and they come with an adjustable elastic headband plus an adjustable light beam. The better quality head torches have varying light levels – lower for baiting the hook and brighter for landing a fish.

Betalites

These are small but tough glass cylinders that contain a gas that emits a green glow. This glow continues for years, only gradually weakening over a decade. They are small enough to be attached to float tops by pieces of silicon rubber.

For your early trips fit them to rod tops for river fishing, (an adapter for this purpose can be purchased from tackle shops) or insert them into 'bobbin' indicators, described below, for still water fishing.

Bobbin indicators

This is a device fastened by a chain or cord to the front rod rest. It hangs on the line between the butt ring (the first ring on the rod above the reel) and the second ring. The indicator itself has an adjustable slot to take the line, which releases when the angler strikes a bite. It also has a recess to take a betalite, and generally hangs on the line some six inches below the rod, lifting towards it as a fish takes line. Your tackle shop staff will be happy to show you these indicators.

Bite alarms

The bite alarm is a small electronic unit screwed into the front rod rest. The rod is normally set in two rests as we have already discussed – one at the rear and one at the front. Bite alarms have a V-shaped aperture to take the rod, which allows the line to ride over the alarm's sensor.

This sensor is activated by movement of the line from a biting fish which causes the alarm to emit a series of 'beeps' and a small light to come on for few seconds. The volume and tone of the beep can be adjusted. Depending on how loud it is it may well awaken an angler who has inadvertently dozed off!

There are two basic types of bite alarms:

- The first has the line running over a small wheel in the alarm. As it turns, it triggers off a response.

- The second works on the same principle as a domestic burglar alarm. Sensors within the unit detect the movement of the line, registering the bite.

A note of caution: If you doze off and you are awakened suddenly by your bite alarm, you may be disorientated. If possible, try to gain some sense of your surroundings before racing towards your rod. Anglers have been known to accidentally jump into the water when dashing from under the brolly to the rod. That's what you call a rude awakening!

Fishing after dark is a completely different environment to coarse fishing in the daytime. For this reason we recommend:

- For your first session accompany a more experienced angler who has previous experience of fishing in the dark. They know what to expect and can provide advice and guidance while you fish.

- Set your tackle up well before dark with your gear and bait close to you, but clear of your feet. Over the years Archie has destroyed spectacles and a good many other items galloping to his rod when an alarm has sounded.

Why is after dark fishing popular with anglers?

In the height of summer, the nights are barely four hours long. At this time of year one of the advantages of staying through the night is to enjoy the spectacular sight of the sun rising on a summer's day, as well as some often glorious sunsets. The full dawn chorus and the world coming back to colour and life is a magical 'event' and the experience is difficult to convey to those who have not experienced it before.

'Even if the fishing is slow, you won't get bored.'

More importantly, from an angling point of view, is the opportunity to observe fish activity at these times. Many species of fish can be observed 'rolling' at the surface of the water both at dawn and dusk.

For the stargazer or nature lover, the after dark experience can open up a whole new world. Many animals lose their caution; voles in particular will sneak up on you unawares, hoping to get their heads into your bait bucket. Owls call back and forth, and bats will also come out and attack the midges which sometimes abound. (Tip: don't forget the insect repellent.) Widgeon, the whistling duck, will also sometimes fly in the dark, making you wonder what that weird noise overhead is.

On clear nights the sky itself puts on a display. It's worth buying a guide to astronomy, as several of the planets are visible at various times of the year; Jupiter, the largest planet in our solar system, is easily observed with the naked eye. Meteor swarms, known to us as shooting stars, are regular occurrences. Even if the fishing is slow, you won't get bored.

What are artificial baits?

In recent years an ever-increasing amount of artificial baits have come onto the market, including boilies, pellets, hemp and even worms. They have been hugely successful and here we'll look at the most popular three.

Maggots

They are produced in several colours, hard ones and soft ones, floaters and sinkers and can be used on the hook direct or on a hair-rig.

- To start with use soft sinkers directly on the hook. When feeder fishing with a quivertip small species of fish can be an outright nuisance, often taking a live maggot almost immediately.

- Often the angler can wind in to find a squashed maggot or sometimes just a skin left on the hook – without the quivertip showing much more than a tremble. That's the time to swap to a rubber maggot, while continuing to fill the feeder with live maggots.

Archie's tip

'Dip your "artificial", already hooked, into your flavour pot prior to casting. Now you know you won't be sitting there biteless if your bait has been crushed or, worse, stolen.'

Casters

Certain species of fish, such as tench, roach and barbel love casters.

- Two casters (also referred to as sinkers) hooked by the extreme ends on a size 16 hook, can bring your swim to life if it has slowed down mid-session. These imitation baits come in shades from pale brown to dark brown, so experiment with different colours until you find out what works best on the day.

Sweetcorn

This artificial bait has been a revelation in angling. It has caught fish everywhere including roach, bream, tench, carp, chub, barbel and more. Current versions are soft enough to fish directly on the hook and they come in different sizes, floaters or sinkers, and various colours. Some anglers use a real corn and a rubber one in conjunction, but that's not often necessary.

'If you only ever try one artificial bait, make it sweetcorn.'

Here's a story which may encourage you if you are unsure about sweetcorn. Archie had a friend who had never tried artificials but was persuaded to try sweetcorn. He went to a busy carp lake, fishing six hours through the middle of the day without using a swimfeeder or a line clip and without putting in any loose feed.

He didn't aim to cast to the same distance as we have suggested in chapter 7. He simply placed a heavy lead on each of his two rods, hooked a single grain of yellow rubber corn on each hook, then cast his rigs as far as he could towards the middle of the lake. His alarms sounded 12 times and he landed 12 mirror carp between 13lbs and 17lbs each. What a day!

The moral of the story is – if you only ever try one artificial bait, make it sweetcorn.

The 'Big Fish Rig'

A cursory glance through the specialist angling magazines will reveal a bewildering array of rigs and end tackles, some of them designed for very specific situations. Don't confuse yourself trying to decide which is best. All you need to do is make up the comparatively simple rig described on the following page, recommended by Archie.

Known as the 'Inline Bolt Rig' it can be used either on still water or rivers and with most baits.

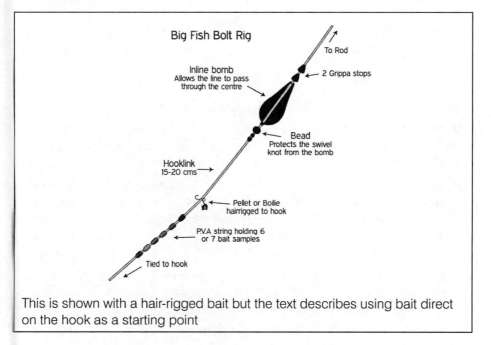

Big Fish Bolt Rig

To Rod

Inline bomb
Allows the line to pass
through the centre

2 Grippa stops

Bead
Protects the swivel
knot from the bomb

Hooklink
15-20 cms

Pellet or Boilie
hairrigged to hook

P.V.A string holding 6
or 7 bait samples

Tied to hook

This is shown with a hair-rigged bait but the text describes using bait direct on the hook as a starting point

How is the Big Fish Rig created?

▨ Thread two rubber float stops onto the line. The best stops for this rig are the Grippa stops supplied by Drennan (details provided in the help list). This is followed by an inline lead which is basically a 'bomb' with a central silicon lined hole through which the line is threaded. The size of the lead is governed by the distance you want to cast, but 2oz is the minimum needed, (3 or 4oz is often used) to ensure the fish hooks itself against the weight.

▨ Next, slide a rubber or plastic bead onto the line, followed by a small swivel which is knotted in place. The bead protects the knot on the swivel from being damaged by the weight of the lead above it.

- Lastly, tie the hooklink to the opposite eye of the swivel, and the basic rig is finished. Because you are hoping for bigger fish, we recommend a 10lb reel line, an 8lb hooklength about 12 inches long and a No 8 eyed hook.

- The hook usually carries a hair-rig, which carries the bait, but for this you need to have mastered the knotless knot (details provided in the appendix). For simplicity we suggest you start by using baits on the hook, covered below.

- The final element is a 'stringer', so called because you thread say seven baits on a piece of string and tie it to the bend of the hook. The difference is that your 'string' is made of PVA, a quick-dissolving material, when immersed in water.

- A soft pellet is used on the hook, and the stringer baits sit in a line below it once cast out. When the PVA dissolves, (two or three minutes at summer water temperatures) you have a line of seven free baits and the baited hook. Your target fish comes along, eats the free offerings and as it can't count it also takes the hookbait – and is hooked.

- Before casting the baited and stringered rig, ensure the lead is sitting comfortably on the bead, and that the two gripper stops are tight against the other side of the lead. The mechanics of this rig are that when the fish takes that booby-trapped eighth bait and turns away, it is pricked by the hook point against the weight of the lead. Startled, it bolts away, driving the hook home, hence the often used term 'Bolt Rig'.

- Although the Grippa stops hold the line tightly, they will slide under pressure. Should the line break on a large fish these stops will slide off the line, dropping the lead off which means the fish is not left tethered to the lead.

- To practise this type of angling requires a bait-runner reel. This is simply a fixed spool reel with an extra function – the ability to feed line freely by just flicking over a lever at the back of the reel once the rod is settled in the rod rests. Without it, a powerful fish could drag your rod from the rests as it bolts. As you pick up the rod to do battle you just flick that lever back again, and you're into normal mode. As Archie says, 'It's all a bit like selecting neutral on a car.'

What bait should be used with the 'Big Fish Rig'?

Any bait that will go on a hook is suitable to use with this rig, such as bunches of maggots, worms, sweetcorn, bread paste, luncheon meat, pellets and so on.

As this stage we have omitted boilies as this would involve various needles, drills and boilie stops. These techniques we are sure you will learn at a later stage in your coarse fishing career. For this reason we suggest you start by buying drilled fishmeal pellets, readily available, to use on the stringer. You will then only need to purchase a stringer needle.

The stringer needle is about six inches long, onto which you thread your seven drilled fishmeal pellets. The small hook on the end of the needle is then used to pull the PVA string through the pellets.

Free the needle and tie the pellets on at both ends of the PVA string, not forgetting to leave a long enough tag at one end to tie the stringer onto the bend of your hook.

Archie's tip

'It's a good idea to tie up a dozen stringers at home and keep them in a waterproof container ready for fishing. It saves a lot of 'fiddly' time on the bank, and perhaps the nightmare of trying to use a water-soluble material in the rain!'

The Big Fish Rig can be taken anywhere, used with almost any bait, and takes a lot of the hard work out of angling, especially for the newcomer.

A final note

The chapters on advanced angling are provided to give you just a flavour of what is possible as you become a more accomplished angler. To cover more advanced rigs would require several more chapters, but we hope this guide has given you a glimpse into the unique world of coarse fishing.

We wish you many successful and enjoyable years with your new hobby.

Summing Up

- After dark angling – or 'night fishing' as it is known, is best tried after gaining confidence and experience with daytime angling. Night fishing introduces another world with a whole host of new experiences for the angler.

- For your first trip, make sure you accompany a more experienced angler. Until you get used to the sights and sounds fishing in the dark can feel a little eerie.

- Additional equipment recommended for after dark angling includes a brolly shelter, head torch, betalites and bite alarms.

- Watch where the fish roll at dawn and dusk and make sure you're in that spot next time you fish.

- Rubber baits prove extremely successful in attracting fish. Maggots, casters and sweetcorn are the most popular but if you select only one make it sweetcorn.

- The big fish rig, or bolt rig, is so called because when the fish picks up the bait, it pricks itself against a heavy lead – and bolts. Anglers who master this basic rig will want to go on to more complicated rigs and ever bigger fish.

Appendix

Knots

In chapter 2 we referred to the three basic knots that you may attempt to master once you have achieved a level of experience in your coarse fishing hobby.

The diagrams below show you these knots.

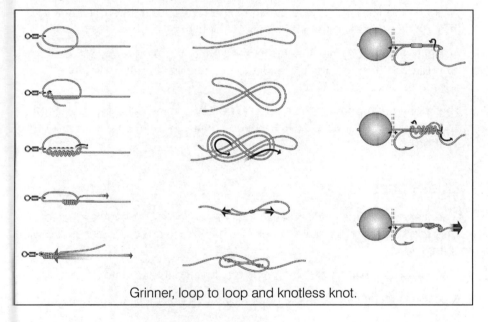

Grinner, loop to loop and knotless knot.

Grinner knot

The best knot for attaching eyed hooks, swivels, rigs and so on.

1. Thread the line twice through the swivel or hook eye.

2. Make a loop and pass the end back through the loop you've made.

3. The tag end should be wrapped around the line seven times.

4. Pass the line through the original loop. When doing this you should make the loop as small as you can.

5. Moisten the knot before sliding it down the swivel/hookeye then pull tight.

Loop to loop knot

1. Fold over your mainline into a loop which you can easily work with.

2. Fold the loop back across itself.

3. Wrap the loop around the back of the folded lines. Next, thread it back through the main loop to form a figure of eight.

4. Adjust the knot size, moisten the line and bring it together. You can do this by pulling on the loop, the tag end and the mainline together. A gentle approach is recommended.

5. The knot you now have can be used to tie loops in the end of a hooklength and mainline which will allow them to be connected using the loop to loop method.

Knotless knot

We mentioned hair-rigs in various sections in the book. This knot is ideal for hair-rigging baits such as boilies when you have gained more experienced with your angling.

1. Place a small piece of silicon tube on the line and thread onto the hook.

2. Next, pass the line through the hook's eye then pull the line down along the hook.

3. Thread the line back through the hookeye and tighten it.

Don't be disheartened if it takes a few attempts to get the technique just right. Tying fishing knots requires nimble fingers and a close eye for detail. With practice and time, however, it becomes second nature to all anglers.

Additional details are also provided in the various fishing magazines and associated websites provided in the help list. If you enter 'coarse fishing hair rigs' into your online search engine under 'Images', you will find a further range of relevant diagrams to choose from

Match fishing

Match fishing is something best attempted when anglers have gained experience. As it is a further specialist area, we have not covered it within this guide.

For anglers wishing to learn about match fishing, for your first step we recommend that you go along and watch a local competition. You can learn a lot from observing other anglers and familiarising yourself with what actually happens on the day.

Glossary

Coarse fishing is full of technical terms and the glossary itself could take up a further chapter. Here we have included some basic terms which we hope will prove useful while reading this book.

Additive

A powder which is used to add flavour to baits with the intention of attracting more fish.

Angling style

A technique used in coarse fishing, such as waggler fishing, margin pole fishing and so on.

Attractor

A liquid or powder substance added to baits or groundbait in the hope of attracting more fish.

Bait dropper

The bait dropper is a device tied to the end of the fishing line and filled with the angler's choice of feed. It is dropped on the bottom of the river during fishing, allowing the contents spill out.

Betalites

These are small but tough glass cylinders containing a gas that emits a green glow. They are used during after dark fishing.

Big Fish Rig

An easy to assemble rig for beginners and anglers with some experience, also referred to as the 'bolt rig'.

Bobbin indicator

This is a device fastened by a chain or cord to the front rod rest to which a betalite can be attached during after dark angling.

Boilies

A modern bait, the boilie is a complex, carefully blended paste rolled into small balls which are then boiled until they are hard enough to deter the attention of smaller fish and remain available for the bigger species.

Bomb fishing

Please refer to leger fishing.

Caster

The chrysalised version of the maggot before it turns into the bluebottle fly. It is a popular bait used by anglers. The preferred shade of caster for bait purposes is light brown.

Casting

Casting is one of the first techniques learned by anglers. It is the art of using the rod to propel, or cast, the end tackle and baited hook into the water.

Disgorger

A simple device which removes the hook safely from the fish's mouth.

End tackle

The general term used to describe the 'business end', i.e. from the lead or float to the hook.

Feeders

A plastic or cylindrical device filled with groundbait or bait. For beginners, two basic feeders are recommended, block end feeders and open end feeders.

Flavours

A liquid attractor which is added to baits to enhance their attractiveness to fish.

Hookbait

This refers to the type of bait selected by the angler to use on the hook.

Hooklength

A short length of line with a hook at one end and a loop or swivel at the other.

Legering

Legering refers to the style of fishing practised where the bait is held on the bottom by a weight, known as a leger weight or bomb. A leger of sufficient weight enables even inexperienced angler to reach much further distances than with a float

Margin pole

A margin pole is used for fishing the water's margins. It is the ideal style of pole fishing for the novice anglers.

Off bottom fishing

This refers to fishing when the bait is held clear off the bottom.

On bottom fishing

This refers to fishing when the bait lies on the bottom.

Pellets

Pellets are modern baits which are basically compressed meals, such as fish meal, provided by the fish farming industry. Pellets come in two forms, hard and soft pellets and have revolutionised the way in which anglers fish in recent times.

Quivertipping

Quivertipping is a style of angling which uses a flexible tip at the end of the rod which is designed to quiver or move when a fish takes the angler's bait.

Rig

Another term used to describe end tackle.

Split-shot

These are shotgun cartridge fillings which have been split open to allow the fishing line to be inserted into them.

Stick float fishing

A specialist style of angling where the float is attached top and bottom. Stick float fishing is generally only carried out on rivers.

Strike

This is the angler's response to the fish taking the bait which enables the hooking of the fish. This is best learned through observation as it is a technique that may take several attempts to master.

Waggler fishing

The term 'waggler fishing' describes float fishing which is carried out by attaching the float to the line by the bottom end only. It can be carried out on any type of water, flowing or still. This slows the progress of the float down the river slightly. The drag also causes the float to waggle slightly from side to side, hence the term 'waggler'.

Help List

There are countless sources of information for those wanting to pursue a hobby in coarse fishing. It is our hope that this selection will provide you with the basic information you need to get started and point you to additional sources as you pursue your new hobby.

It is impossible to include every angling source or website so apologies are due to any that have been inadvertently omitted. All details are correct at time of writing.

National sources of information

England and Wales

Environment Agency

www.environment-agency.gov.uk/homeandleisure/recreation/fishing/
National Customer Contact Centre, PO Box 544, Rotherham S60 1BY
General Enquiries: 03708 506 506 (Mon-Fri, 8am-6pm)
The Environment Agency has a dedicated section on coarse fishing with a wealth of information for anyone covering England and Wales. This includes details of where to purchase your rod licence and a complete list of fisheries and fishing events. The information is now regularly updated online.
This is an essential source for all anglers in England and Wales.

Northern Ireland

Loughs Agency

www.loughs-agency.org
22 Victoria Road, Derry-Londonderry, Northern Ireland, BT47 2AB
Tel : 02871 342100
The Loughs Agency is an agency of the Foyle, Carlingford and Irish Lights Commission (FCILC), established as one of the cross-border bodies under the 1998 Agreement between the government of the United Kingdom of Great

Britain and Northern Ireland and the government of Ireland. The Agency aims to provide sustainable social, economic and environmental benefits through the effective conservation, management, promotion and development of the fisheries and marine resources of the Foyle and Carlingford Areas.
Details of loughs and fisheries are provided on this site, together with information on permits/licences.

Northern Ireland Government Services

Northern Ireland's starting point and primary source of information for those wishing to pursue a coarse fishing hobby. The website links below cover general angling information, details of licences and permits and an online source to purchase your licences.

www.nidirect.gov.uk/index/information-and-services/leisure-home-and-community/leisure-and-recreation/outdoor-recreation/angling.htm

www.nidirect.gov.uk/index/information-and-services/leisure-home-and-community/leisure-and-recreation/outdoor-recreation/angling/game-and-coarse-angling/angling-licence-and-permit-prices.htm

www.nidirect.gov.uk/index/do-it-online/leisure-home-and-community-online/buy-angling-licences-and-permits.htm

www.nidirect.gov.uk/where-can-i-fish-in-northern-ireland

Scotland

Scottish Federation for Coarse Angling

www.sfca.co.uk
The governing body for coarse fishing in Scotland.
E-mail contact information is provided on the website.

Fishing gear and tackle supplies

Dragon Carp Direct/Used Tackle

www.usedtackledirect.co.uk
www.dragoncarpdirect.com
Dragon Carp Direct, Unit 3, Calow Land Industrial Estate, Chesterfield,
Derbyshire S41 0DR
Tel : 01246 540140
sales@dragoncarpdirect.com
An excellent source of cost-effective fishing gear providing everything for the
novice angler, from tiny hooks to powerful rods at extremely competitive prices.
Special thanks to Roger Surgay at Dragon Carp Direct/Used Tackle and Steve
Partner, Editorial Director at Strike One Media for providing several photos
used within this book.

Drennan International

www.drennantackle.com
Recommended supplier for the use of the shoulder stick float and Grippa
stops mentioned in chapters 8 and 10 respectively.

Magazines and newspapers

In addition to the national publications listed below, most national and regional
newspapers will have a regular dedicated angling column.

Angler's Mail

www.anglersmail.co.uk
Angler's Mail, 9th Floor, Blue Fin Building, 110 Southwark Street, London, SE1
0SU
Tel: 0203 148 4159
anglersmail@ipcmedia.com

Bauer Media

www.bauermedia.co.uk
Bauer Consumer Media Ltd
1 Lincoln Court, Lincoln Rd, Peterborough PE1 2RF

Bauer Media is responsible for the following publications:

Angling Times

www.gofishing.co.uk/Angling-Times
Tel: 01733 395108

Improve Your Coarse Fishing

www.gofishing.co.uk/Angling-Times/Section/Improve-Your-Coarse-Fishing
Tel: 01733 395138

UK Carp

Tel: 01733 395104

www.gofishing.co.uk

The website has a number of videos available offering a wealth of advice to anglers.

Record British Fish

www.gofishing.co.uk/Angling-Times/Section/News--Catches/British-fish-record-weights/Coarse-Fish-Records

Coarse Angling Today

www.coarseanglingtoday.co.uk
Predator Publications Ltd, Newport East, Yorkshire HU15 2QG
Tel: 01430 440624

Additional resources

Angling Projects

www.angling-projects.org.uk
Les Webber, MBE
5 Walnut Way, Tilehurst, Reading, Berkshire RG30 4TD
Tel: 0118 945 1701
As quoted on their website and mentioned in the introduction to this guide, Angling Projects has gained an enviable reputation throughout the UK as being one of the best facilities for groups of young anglers in the country. This facility is open free of charge to groups of youngsters from the age of 8 years upwards, including groups from schools, youth clubs, scouts/guide groups, junior angling clubs and children at risk and with special needs and disabilities.

Angling Trust

www.anglingtrust.net
Eastwood House, 6 Rainbow Street, Leominster, Herefordshire HR6 8DQ
Tel: 0844 7700 616
The Angling Trust is an organisation which aims to protect the interests of all coarse, sea and game anglers in England. Website links are available to help anglers find a tackle shop, club, fishery and coach.

British Disabled Angling Association

www.bdaa.co.uk
9 Yew Tree Road, Delves, Walsall, West Midlands, WS5 4NQ
Tel : 01922 860912
The British Disabled Angling Association is a charity which develops opportunities for people of all ages and abilities to access the activity of fishing in the UK.

Get Hooked On Fishing

www.ghof.org.uk
Contact details for each national project are provided on the website.
A charitable organisation which runs an angling programme helping to provide positive opportunities for young people and communities.

The Met Office

www.metoffice.gov.uk/weather/uk/uk_forecast_weather.html
An ideal website to check your local weather forecast which will enable you to plan your fishing trip.

The Post Office

www.postoffice.co.uk/rod-fishing-licence

www.postoffice.co.uk/branch-finder
The above links will enable you to find your local post office branch where you can purchase your rod licence in England and Wales.

Book List

Archie Braddock's Magic Book on Bait Flavouring
Archie still has a few copies left for anglers interested in purchasing this book.
Archie Braddock
21 Elgar Drive
Long Eaton
Nottingham NG10 3PY
Tel: 0115 972 6886

Archie Braddock's Fantastic Feeder Fishing
Sadly, this is no longer in print but a quick search online revealed a number of websites where second hand copies can still be purchased.